Other books by Ann

Confessions of a Knitting Heretic
(ModeKnit Press, 2002)

Knitting Millinery
(ModeKnit Press, 2004)

Cheaper Than Therapy
(ModeKnit Press, 2005)

Twist & Loop
(Potter Craft, 2006)

Men Who Knit
[& the Dogs Who Love Them]
(Lark / Sterling, 2006)

Romantic Hand Knits
(Potter Craft, 2007)

Flip Knits
[Knit, Purl, Increase, Decrease]
(ModeKnit Press, 2007)

FOR GERRY, HANNAH & MAX

Knit with Courage, Live with Hope

A Year in Saint Paul

BY

Annie Modesitt

Published by ModeKnit Press
140 Lexington Parkway South
St. Paul, MN 55105

Special thanks to Lissy Friedman for her excellent help in proofreading and editing this work.

All photographs were taken by the author, with the exception of the publicity still on page 46 for The Incredible Shrinking Man (©1957 Universal International Pictures) which has been artistically altered by the author.

The images shown at the start of each month are architectural details from the Plummer Building at the Mayo Clinic Complex, Rochester, MN.

The image at the start of September is a detail from a carving at the Cathedral of Saint-Nazaire in Beziers, France.

The "hope bone" bead pictured on pg 148 was created by Judy Fearn, a member of the International Society of Glass Beadmakers. The bead is flameworked and kiln annealed in her Minnesota studio.

Knit with Courage, Live with Hope

A Year in Saint Paul
2007

Special Thanks

There are so many people to thank over this past year that the list would be longer than this book itself.

Outstanding in our daily lives have been many new (and old) friends who allowed us to live a relatively *"normal"* life while fighting the battle of our lives.

Thank you, Alison, Catherine, Lisa, Devi, Uli, Andrea, John, Ian, Coco, Nancy, John, Jim, London, Beth, Elaine, Jan, Gayle, Ellyn, Judy, Cora, Jane, Athena, Laurie, Ami, Judy, Kathleen, Elise, Paula, Susan, Polly, Eve, Sou, Lucille, Janine, Janice, A, Elizabeth, Rocksolana, Marie, Vanessa, Zoebelle, Zoebelle, Nicolette, Norah, Ivete, Ferrons, Nancys, Cynthia, Nancy, Karen, EMMA, Mike, Annemarie, Elizabeth, Luise, Rebecca, Joanne, Cynthia, Benne, Susan, Teri, Mary, Sheri, Marianne, Iris, Julie, Nancy, Ellen, Irene, Cecilia, Erica, Linda, Staci, French, Eliz, Karin, Anne, June, michelle, Margaret, Leslie, Ileana, Susan, Dorothy, Joanne, Melinda, Dawn, Marin, Brandy, Kate, Robin, Colleen, Donna, Delia, Margaret, Rosemary, Deirdre, Kathleen, Nancy, Leigh, Kamala, Kristen, Paget, Jane, Susan, Chris, Teresa, Susan, Leah, RedLipstick, Minnie, Thomas, Cecilia, Martha, varia, Ellyn, Dee, Megan, Helen, Heather, Wen, Anna, Anne, Amie, Mary, Shannon, David, Barbara, Carol, Nancy, Jenny, Lisa, Pamela, carrie, Donna, Desiree, Joy, Looped, Halina, Erin, Wilma, Janice, Anna, Judith, Amber, Danita, Alison, Heather, Kathleen, Marsha, Sheryl, Karen, Nicola, Alice, Truth, Susan, Izabela, Jennifer, Joan, Ann, Kristen, mindi, Jennifer, Jennifer, robin, Sandra, Nell, Jan, Amanda, Roseann, Lee, ruby, James, Knitting, Barbara, Denise, sandra, Barbara, Julia, Poise.cc, Maureen, Mary, Rhoda, Susan, Margaret, Stephanie, Stephanie, Laura, Wendy, Knitty, Lucinda, Charlotte, Heather, LuAnne, Minx, ann, Sherri, Linda, Deborah, Nan, Janet, Victoria, Jocelyne, Deborah, Lea, Cathy, Tracey, Diane, Margaret, Melise, Knit, Jodi, Simply, Marylen, Wendy, William, Rachel, Jessica, Judith, Deann, Kathleen, Susan, DiscountYarnSale.com, Kimberly, Sheri, Kate, Melanie, Tina, Jennifer, Catherine, Kelly, Kate, Linda, Leslie, mary, Make, Linda, Julia, JoAnne, Aimee, Deborah, Frederica, Marnie, Michelle, Cindy, the Millionaire & his Wife, the Movie star... & the rest...

Keeping a journal is a private affair, but blogging is about as public as one can get. My blog started as a way to describe the *Daily Life of a Hand Knit Designer,* with small personal bits interspersed between the stitch patterns and technique tips.

But a funny thing happened when my husband developed Multiple Myeloma, a terminal *(terminal? Life is terminal!)* blood cancer that affects the bone marrow. The blog took on a more intimate role and became key not just in how I but our entire family dealt with the changes we were facing.

I have been keeping my blog since 2002, writing several times a week – sometimes daily – but it wasn't until my husband's illness that I realized how broad and deep the community of blog readers had become.

With very few exceptions, the comments and emails generated by my blog have been kind, supportive and one of the best aspects of a difficult situation.

Knowing I'll be writing about certain situations, about my feelings and interactions, makes it easier to get through some of the harder parts in life.

And the fun parts, too. If life isn't about having fun and finding joy in unexpected places, then what's the point? Reading about other folks' adventures, writing about my own, it's a connection that I enjoy making – especially in the fiber community.

Most especially, the warm embrace that my whole family has felt has been a great comfort in this past year. There are days that are very hard – times when I'm away from home, away from Gerry and the kids, and I find my mind wandering to the scary place where I ask, *"Is this what it will be like when..?"*

I don't go there often, and seldom on purpose. But I'm human, and I can't help but ponder the future. I can't help but tie myself up in a ribbon of *"What If's"*— as silly as that is.

Silly, but human.

We all think those things, I have the perspective of understanding that I [we] may be closer to the not-to-be-considered future than I once thought I was. We are.

But this type of pondering doesn't take center stage very often. It's more like the pattern on the wallpaper or the weave of a carpet. It's there, and I can get lost in the design if I let myself. Or I can allow it to augment our lives, bring a different understanding to every day events and make everything that we do that much sweeter.

I do have my breakdown moments. Usually not in front of anyone — *except, perhaps, a class of 20 people in Austin, TX.* But for the most part I'm happier keeping the sorrow to myself, secure in the knowledge that if I need support in those times, I'll find it in my friends.

Because this is a day-by-day journal of a year as it unfolds, some tenses may seem odd — present tenses used to describe incidents which have already happened. Remember as you read this that it is a record of the year 2007 as our family experienced it, with corrections made later to make the narrative easier to follow.

I'm continuously surprised and gratified at how many friendships have been built through my blog, I can't imagine getting through this without them.

We are grateful to everyone who has reached out to us, and to the many folks who simply, quietly read along with our lives and send us good thoughts. Thank you!

Annie Modentt

January

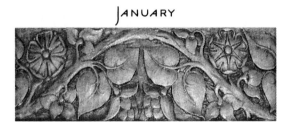

JANUARY FIRST
DO-OVER
SOUTH ORANGE, NJ

So we have our timeline – I'll be flying to San Diego, then I'll meet Gerry who is flying to the Twin Cities to look at our finalist houses. And we will make a decision. Then back home for the two week marathon of packing. This whole move to Minnesota has happened so quickly. As I flew into the Minneapolis/St. Paul airport last April I looked out the window and felt oddly at home.

Arriving in a new town to teach techniques to knitters and crocheters allows me to meet a small, but very broad, cross section of the population. I usually have many more women than men in my classes, but they cut across all race, age, income and religious strata, and this gives me an interesting perspective on the places where I teach.

My impression of the Twin Cities was so positive that I joked to my classes, *"I'm thinking of moving here..."* But I wasn't joking. Jennie the Potter, a friend I made my first day in town, gave me a full tour of Minneapolis and St. Paul, and by dinner I'd called Gerry to tell him we HAD to put our house in New Jersey on the market.

It wasn't so much that Minneapolis/St. Paul was the best place I'd been to (it's up there). Rather, it's the comfort level I immediately felt here – a sense that my family belonged in this diverse-yet-homogenous community where folks simply will NOT accept a poor standard of living.

And there was something more – a strong push, some nagging feeling, that we MUST move here. I joked that my late mother was on one shoulder and my late brother on the other yelling in my ear, "MOVE, *damnit*."

But at the time I just figured it was the rising property taxes in our beloved South Orange, NJ and my Gerry's desperate unhappiness at his job that gave us the push. The strongest shove of all though, was how deeply I fell in love with this area in my week of teaching in Minneapolis/St. Paul.

I am NOT an "everything happens for a reason" person – I don't believe that. But I do think that there is *some* reason we need to be in Minnesota now, even if the reason is just a higher standard of living for our kids.

In April I first *met* Minneapolis; in August our family flew in and spent a week north of the Twin Cities on a look-and-see vacation; in September in New Jersey we put our house on the market and it sold in a little less than two months. The closing is scheduled for February, so we'd better find a house.

Not having a place to live in MN is a little scary, but if worst comes to worst we'll rent a home for a bit. At the end of January I'm off to Chicago to teach, back to South Orange for more packing, then off to Rochester, NY for more classes the weekend before our move. Gerry's stuck with the final packing and sending off of the PODS – nice how I worked that...

There are so many things to think about; I'm hoping Gerry can step it up and get more of the lifting and packing done while I'm away. I've never been so exhausted in my life, and we're not even started!

I'm noticing that Gerry is hesitant about the packing, so I'm picking up the slack. He's not usually so foot-dragging about physical labor, it makes me wonder if there's something going on.

JANUARY FIFTEENTH
IF IT'S MONDAY, IT MUST BE MINNESOTA
ST. PAUL, MN

I lost my iPod in San Diego at TNNA. I could cry. Traveling is hard; trying to remember the "intelligent" places you've stored stuff is impossible. I half expect to get home and find my little iPod in my luggage.

But I have other things on my mind now. Specifically, the House Of Our Dreams. We both loved it – we saw

the drawbacks – and we still love it. We were the third couple to bid on this house and it had only been on the market for five days.

It's absolutely lovely, warm, inviting; there's an excellent floor plan and room for an office. The down side is it only has a one-car garage, a very tiny yard, and the initial unpacking/unloading is going to be EVIL hard.

Now the real work starts, the MOVE. Gerry's back has been very sore lately – he was barely able to move last weekend – so we may be hiring guys to pack and move. I can't do it all myself. Gerry left to go back to South Orange this afternoon, I'll fly back tomorrow evening. According to the weather forecast it's supposed to warm up tomorrow. It may hit 25° F. *Above* zero!

4

JANUARY SEVENTEENTH
THE RETURN OF THE NON-NATIVE
ST. PAUL, MN

Here in St. Paul many folks assume I'm a native New Jersey girl. It can't be the accent (do I have one?). Perhaps it's my attitude? It's time to work on wrapping my knee-jerk frankness in a blanket of niceness so I'm not such an easy tell in Minnesota.

I moved to New Jersey when I was in grad school at Rutgers in New Brunswick. Before I lived here I had many of the same odd, unflattering and erroneous attitudes about Jersey that the rest of the country seems to have. I hadn't realized how wonderful this state is, how beautiful, historic, full of natural FUN. It's an amazing place and we've been lucky to live here.

It's a wonderful dilemma to love several places so much! Just about everywhere I've lived has been a fascinating and entertaining place. And now we're off to Minnesota.

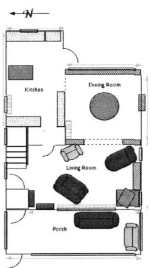

Back in St. Paul, as I was walking around our new neighborhood and feeling a tiny bit at home, I realized how much it feels like Brooklyn Heights – a very, very "nice" Brooklyn Heights.

JANUARY NINETEENTH
GRAND PLAN
SOUTH ORANGE, NJ

Being a Virgo – and Dutch – planning is one of my strengths. I love to spend time arranging, estimating, measuring, creating conditional options. I would have made a terrific Quartermaster.

Last night as I was getting ready for bed I started working up a floorplan of the new house, based on the photos I took and my unscientific "shoe" measure. Seeing a floorplan makes me calm, it helps me feel secure that our furniture WILL fit, that we WILL be able to enjoy and appreciate a slightly smaller house, and that we won't feel cramped.

But I feel so much stress. After all, I am the impetus for this move, I'm the reason we're packing up and traveling halfway across the country. And I'm not entirely sure why. It feels so – right – but in this day and age is a feeling enough? Gerry trusts me, but should he?

And with stress comes paralysis. I know I should be packing boxes, working on designs and preparing for my next teaching trip. But all I want to do is sit and stare at the beautiful snow outside. Mentally, I'm raring to go. Physically, I need another day to decompress after this past week. And I need to stop fretting over things that I can't control.

JANUARY TWENTIETH

THE PITCH

SOUTH ORANGE, NJ
"Life is a casting off."

– Linda Loman,
Death of a Salesman

Who knew that Linda was a knitter? I'm casting off. Throwing out. Pitching. Deciding what we need and what we don't. Yesterday while the kids were at school I went through their closets and tossed EVERYTHING that doesn't fit anymore. FOUR bags of Goodwilldestined garments and a few bags of garbage later, I felt that I'd done a good days' work.

I'm answering emails, filling book orders, arranging travel for my spring gigs and doing general computer housecleaning. Necessary, but not very thrilling. After I finish that, I'm rewarded with the very exciting job of packing our fine china. Life on the edge.

JANUARY TWENTY–SECOND
LETTING GO
SOUTH ORANGE, NJ

Today I spent a good part of the afternoon in my basement office pitching old files that I haven't used or even LOOKED at in the past 4 years – old, old stuff – knowing in my soul that the minute the garbage is carted away, I'll need one of those files.

Perhaps the best six-word excuse in history: "I lost that when I moved..."

Gerry and I confessed our fantasies to each other this evening while he was making rice and I was putting away yogurt. *Sounds kinky, n'est ce pas?*

Well, it's not. We both have the same deep seated desire to break the back kitchen wall out of our new house and expand the kitchen.

However, Gerry's been suffering with a bad back for about three weeks. Today he finally went to the back doctor and had some X-rays. He's tight – that's the official, initial diagnosis. So he's supposed to do physical therapy two to three times a week, and he wants to see an acupuncturist.

I've been trying to work out a pattern for a kimono style swing coat but I haven't been able to find a comfort level with my gauge swatch. I think I'll sleep with it tonight. Wouldn't it be nice if that were Gerry's fantasy?

JANUARY TWENTY-FOURTH
POD People
SOUTH ORANGE, NJ

They're coming tomorrow.

We received a cryptic phone call alerting us that between 6:00 a.m. and 9:00 a.m. the PODS will arrive.

Be afraid, be very afraid...

Fear #1 The PODS Won't Fit Down Our Driveway.

Fear #2 So Where Will We Put The Dumpster?

Fear #3 St. Paul PODS Permit. Hard to Get?

Fear #4 How will I keep Gerry from being "brave" and packing stuff while I'm away in Chicago?

(However, given his recent inclination to not pack, it's probably not an issue...)

JANUARY TWENTY-FIFTH
Had Pod-Ya
SOUTH ORANGE, NJ

So my worrying wasn't misplaced.

Apparently the POD CANNOT get to our backyard. Instead of having two PODS on our driveway, and loading them at the same time, we'll have just one. We'll load it up, send it off, and then have POD2 delivered. I was a bit stymied at first by this change in plans, but it is what it is.

Once POD2 is taken away, we will experience The Return Of The Dumpster. Yes, in a limited return engagement, direct from Mauriello Bros Waste Management and playing to packed houses across New Jersey, the DUMPSTER will be back on Irving Avenue again. Seating is limited.

The hardest part today? Packing my yarn and [gulp] a few cases of finished garments onto the POD. Scary. This is my living, all this yarn. Can I trust the POD?

We had intended to rent a trailer from U-Haul. It sounds so innocuous, huh? Rent a trailer. Nothing could be easier, right? Well, somehow Gerry and I both made it to mid adulthood without realizing that you can't rent a trailer if you *don't have a trailer hitch!*

Getting the hitch seems to be almost as expensive as renting the trailer, so we're rethinking our plan. We may be sending a whole lot more in the second POD than originally intended...

January Twenty-Sixth
Stronger, Longer
South Orange, NJ

This is what I packed yesterday in POD1.

It may not look like much, but it is. Touch me! And that's why my own back and legs are a-hurtin' today.

So today as I sit and blog (and answer email, and write patterns, and generally get myself ready to go teach this coming week), there are two strong men carrying boxes out to POD1, packing things up, and basically doing the work of, well, *one* strong woman.

9

On a TV show a man was complaining about his back. His kids asked his wife, *"Mommy, why does Daddy's back hurt so much?"* She replied, *"Because he thought of it first..."*

I'm feeling that way, and it's not pretty.

FEBRUARY

F<small>EBRUARY</small> S<small>EVENTH</small>
R<small>OOTS &</small> L<small>EAVES</small>
S<small>OUTH</small> O<small>RANGE</small>, NJ

We've lived on Irving Avenue nine and a half years. Hannah was eleven months old when we moved here, and Max was born a few months later.

Not long after that I ordered two trees online, and two

little sticks arrived in the mail. Twigs, barely as thick as my thumb. Our elm and mimosa trees. We planted the elm in the backyard, we planted the mimosa in the front, and they have flourished.

Folks are astonished that the mimosa is only about five years old, it's tall, but spare, and in the summer it has nice leaf coverage. There were eight blossoms last year and I was hoping that there would be many more this year. Mimosa's are considered a "noxious weed" in Minnesota, I guess we'll have no mimosa's there...

The elm is a slower grower, but it's doing well. It's maybe 15' tall now, fully shaped with that lovely elm tree silhouette. It's a special disease resistant breed, the only thing Dutch here is me.

We've put down some very deep roots in nine years, and it's heartbreaking to be leaving. It's a good move, positive in almost every way, but heartbreaking. When the inspector came into our home a few days ago she casually remarked, *"Beautiful home!"* and I burst into tears.

Many friends have spoken longingly of going with us to St. Paul. It's easier to express admiration for the North Star State when the wind chill here in NJ is below zero. Gerry and the kids will struggle through this weekend on air mattresses with paper plates and plastic cups.

I'll be in a nice, soft bed in Rochester, NY. Today more boxes arrive, and while I'm gone, Gerry will finish packing. Or not. His back has been SO painful that he missed work a few days this week to rest, the timing of this sucks, but there's not a lot that can be done besides rest a bad back!

February Eleventh
Vacation from Bedlam
Rochester, NY

I'm feeling very guilty this morning. I slept last night in a soft, lovely, white, fluffy bed that was actually more than 4" off the floor (no air mattress here!). I was lulled to sleep by a fire in the fireplace and a cup of tea.

Perhaps guilty isn't the word, I don't really *believe* in feeling guilty for an extended period. Guilt should be like a fire alarm, compelling us to address a situation and move on. So maybe the way I'll address this spasm of guilt will be to get our fireplace in St. Paul up to working order?

I guess I don't feel entirely guilty that I have a carpet under my feet (ours left in the POD last week). Just having a few hours away from the packing and loading is quite a luxury.

Before I left I taped together all of the remaining boxes. The master plan is for Gerry to not lift or carry anything, just to pack stuff up and leave it to be carried

13

away by the Four Strong Guys From Irvington who will be coming on Tuesday.

I changed my Tuesday flight from 1:00 p.m. to 6:30 a.m. so I'll arrive home first thing in the morning and will be able to give Gerry a bit of a break. I miss him so much when I'm on the road.

FEBRUARY TWELFTH

MIDNIGHT ROCHESTER MUSINGS

ROCHESTER, NY

My flight tomorrow is at 6:30 a.m., I have a 4:45 a.m. wake up call, but I can't fall asleep.

It floors me how different each class, each region, each shop, has such a unique personality. One is not necessarily better than another, it's chemistry (which is why we each gravitate to different shops!).

The chemistry this weekend here in Rochester was phenomenal! I gave a lecture to The Rochester Knitting Guild tonight, the room was full – I seldom speak to such a large group – and they were SO attentive! It was one of my better lectures and I was thrilled to show off my knitting and sign a bunch of books after the talk was over.

My publicist from Sterling called today to say that I'm scheduled for a book signing at the Mall of America in Minnesota on Saturday at 4:00 p.m., and another on Sunday at 1:00 p.m.. Well, there's a reason to make it to St. Paul by Friday.

I can't believe that this time tomorrow we'll be spending my last night in the home we've grown to love so much.

February Fourteenth

Gerry & Annie's Excellent Adventure

Somewhere in Central PA

February 14th, the day of the great 2007 Valentine's Day Nor'easter that swept most of Pennsylvania and New Jersey. And our moving day. Up at 2:30 a.m., worried about moving in the midst of sleeting snow and ice.

I sent an email to our attorney and real estate agent outlining a few scenarios which would allow us to deal with mother nature in a more graceful way, but it didn't make me feel any better.

I started packing up both cars around 7:00 a.m. and then I got on the phone to our garage clean-out company (they were scheduled to remove the residual garage stuff today). I rescheduled them to do it after the Winter storm is over. It's become obvious that the dumpster blocking the garage is going nowhere during this storm, and the storm is due to last through Friday.

By 10:30 a.m. we were good to go – and let me tell you there ain't nothin' as much fun as packing two cars and rooftop storage units in a NOR'EASTER. My hands are still red and burning two days later.

Of course, the folks buying our house insisted on their noon walk-through as scheduled, at NOON, storm or no storm. We were later told they'd been terribly annoyed at the snowy footprints in the house. It's refreshing to see that they won't let a little thing like a Winter storm get in the way of moving.

Ironically, we'd moved the closing back a day to accommodate our buyers so they could be in the house to celebrate Shabbat by sundown on Friday. Unfortunately, allowing us a few extra hours in the middle of a Winter storm to pack the cars wasn't an option. What am I missing?

And Gerry's back is more painful than ever. It seems the physical therapy may have made whatever is wrong worse.

After stopping by the bank and our attorney's office, we left South Orange. Farewell, New Jersey. In retrospect we probably should have just checked into a motel and waited out the storm, but we were all packed and thought that if we could get to Pennsylvania we could outrun it. Famous last words.

The roads were iffy-but-good from NJ to PA, then they suddenly got TERRIBLE 50 miles into the state. We sat in bumper to bumper traffic (just us and trucks) for almost an hour, waiting to get off at an exit for a hotel. We were lucky, many folks spent 17 hours in their cars at that same point in the highway.

Both cars almost had accidents; Gerry spun 180° and I spun 240° at different points on the highway. Luckily traffic was going about five mph, so it was more of a ballet with cars than potential accident, and no damage was done. The kids were terrified, though. When we finally made it off the highway (the exit ramps were worse than the roads), we limped to a Holiday Inn Express and we were told that we just missed the last room. We almost cried. Actually, I did cry.

Then the REALLY nice guy at the desk told us they were cleaning another room and we could have it. We

REALLY got the last one. Later Gerry and I wondered if he said that to everyone... I don't care if he did, I gave him a tip.

No food. The hotel didn't have a restaurant and the town officially closed at 6:00 p.m. No Wendy's or Micky D's or even a 7-11. We scammed instant oatmeal and old bananas from the breakfast room, and brought the pets in with tacit approval from the nice guy at the front desk. (He said he'd already let one dog in, so as long as we promised they'd stay in their crates, we'd be okay... Tipping is a good thing.) We feel like the luckiest folks in the world.

Now if only we weren't so hungry.

FEBRUARY FIFTEENTH

BEATING THE STORM

SOMEWHERE IN INDIANA

We left our safe haven at 10:00 a.m. and drove very slowly until about noon, when the road magically became clear and we were able to drive the speed limit of 65 mph. A few stops for grub and we decided that we'd drive until one of us called the other on our cell phones and said, *"UNCLE!"*

It's 11:00 p.m. and we're in Indiana somewhere. We almost stayed in Toledo, but I protested and de-registered us from the flea bag that had no internet. Our Motel 8 in Indiana is light years better than the flea bag.

I got pulled over by a cop on the access road to the flea bag. An isolated, empty, country road which dead-ended into a "no outlet" cul-de-sac. I stopped at a stop sign, turned left at the dead end, and immediately a cop was on my butt with lights flashing. Apparently he felt I had

17

NOT stopped. But I had. But he didn't "see" me stop. He did, however, see my NJ license plate.

He let me go with a warning to *"Be more careful, ma'am."* I will be more careful. I'll avoid flea bags in Toledo. Speaking as a native Toledoan, sometimes this part of the world is a little odd.

Tomorrow we should arrive in St. Paul in time for dinner.

February Seventeenth
Snow Drive
St. Paul, MN

We arrived in St. Paul around 6:00 p.m. on Friday, unloaded and filled up the air mattresses. I had a minor meltdown – stress from the road and too much time with a pre-teen who tends to think that everything "sucks."

While Gerry and the kids had pizza, I crashed.

The highlight of the day – a low-key highlight, I don't think we had the energy for anything else – was the Linwood Boosters skating party. Most beautiful was the sleigh ride around Linwood park. The view up from the top of the hill was so lovely, and made me feel less lonesome for the beautiful view at the top of the hill back home in NJ.

Home to crawl into bed together and watch *Young Frankenstein* on our laptop. The kids enjoyed it, I fell asleep, Gerry's back hurt.

He said, *"My back is KILLING me!"* like Peter Boyle and the kids laughed.

February Eighteenth
St. Paul Sunday
St. Paul, MN

My first Sunday as an official St. Paul resident, and I feel a break in the stress of the past few days. Emotionally I'm a bit of a wreck. I think I should just go off into a room and cry for a few hours, then come out and wash my face and move on.

I chalk this up to several factors, tops among them:

- I haven't been able to knit much lately.
- I'm tired.
- My knees hurt.
- Gerry's back hurts *(like hell)*.
- I have two deadlines looming and I'm scared.

Lesser on the list, but still worrisome are:

- Will the kids like their schools?
- Will Gerry find a doctor he likes and heal his back?
- Will I make the mortgage each month (now that it's all on my back)?
- Will I need a doctor to heal my back?

Basically, the universal worries that everyone has.

So today I was the first one up and headed out for a walk to a nearby Caribou Coffee for free Wifi and some me time. Time on my own when no one needs anything from me – mentally, physically, organizationally or emotionally – for a few minutes. I leave on Thursday to teach three days in Tampa, and I must say that it will be a relief to leave some of the moving stress behind me.

Last week Gerry and I read an email that made us both cry. The Minnesota Knitters Guild will be putting together a roster of knitters to come by and help us unpack next week. It's hard to explain how welcome this assistance is, coming just when we need it.

FEBRUARY NINETEENTH

LIVE FROM LEXINGTON PARKWAY

ST. PAUL, MN

I'm sitting on the floor in what will be the upstairs office/media room/kids hangout area in our new house, and I'm ON THE INTERNETS! We have cable *(we've never had cable)* and I have a crazy, wacky feeling that I will NEVER turn C-Span off. *I feel an addiction coming on...*

We dropped off 50 pounds of dirty clothing yesterday at the Sel-Dale Laundry. Today they had everything washed, folded, wrapped in bundles of plastic with shirts on hangers, all for the bargain price of $1 per pound. As I was driving to pick up our laundry I was filled with such a feeling of well-being.

The view of the state capital from Selby doesn't hurt, either – it was quite beautiful this morning. I feel certain that we will be happy here.

FEBRUARY TWENTY-FIRST

TAKING 5

ST. PAUL, MN

Both PODS arrived this morning; we have movers coming in about 15 minutes to unload them. I already did a good bit of pre-unloading, getting stuff stacked in piles of what will go to what room, etc., and have thus earned myself an afternoon of knitting.

The house is cluttered (of course...) but it's an organized clutter. There are boxes everywhere, but the boxes are where they need to be. As a special gift to us, St. Paul has arranged to have spring-like weather this week so we can unpack and settle in without frostbite. I don't know if we'll be seeing any crocuses in the next day or so, but this weekend it's supposed to get messy with rain and snow again. *C'est la vie*!

I tried out our routine this morning, walking Hannah to her school at 8:00 a.m., then returning to the same corner to drop off Maxie for his bus at 8:45 a.m. I'm not sure why their schedules are so different but it may work out nicely, that extra half hour in the morning with Max.

I was wondering if it was a good idea to split the kids, but Max was much chattier, more independent than he usually is as we walked to his bus stop. I think he will really dig being an "only child" at school.

There's just so much to do. Today we chose a clinic and Gerry has an appointment for Monday for his back. I'll wait until I get back on Saturday to make my appointment for my legs. Both of us are so sore.

Our insurance will carry over through June 2008 (it's Gerry's union insurance. Yay, union!), so that gives us a bit of breathing room until Gerry finds an insurance-providing job. With his back so sore, that may take more time than we'd considered.

FEBRUARY TWENTY–SIXTH
GOOD NEIGHBORS
ST. PAUL, MN

Thank heavens for our neighbors.

We couldn't get our snowplow started this morning, so we walked down our neighbors' freshly plowed sidewalk and asked them if we could borrow their plow to clear our small area of sidewalk.

Our kind neighbor made the first cut down our sidewalk through the two feet of snow, and after a brief lesson I finished the job and cleared off the area in front of our garage. Long live the snow blower.

I could tell that Gerry felt terrible that he couldn't do more – he was in total agony. What IS up with his darned back? His doctor visit is tomorrow and not a moment too soon!

Later in the day I finished off the area in front of the garage by hand, then moved our other car in front of the garage so it's off the street. I'm not entirely certain of the snow route rules, so we figure the best bet is to just get the car off the street if possible until it's all clear. Apparently the kids have school tomorrow. Should I be surprised that a little snow – *22 inches being "a little" in Minnesota* – doesn't stop the school system?

Tomorrow is also the day the knitting guild friends are coming by to help us unpack so I need to get organized. The closet issue will also have to be dealt with – there just aren't enough for us to have our clothes as we did in NJ, so we'll have to do a lot more folding than we did before. Paring down is a good thing, but it's hard.

FEBRUARY TWENTY–SEVENTH
WRENCHING PAIN

ST. PAUL, MN

On the good side, life is going very well for both kids, they like their schools, the other kids and they're settling in wonderfully. I had a lovely visit from some MN knitting guild friends who came by yesterday with food and helping hands to get my yarn straightened up, and

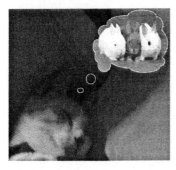

Ninotchka is on TV today. I get to introduce Hannah to one of my favorite movies.

But we've had some great pain.

Gerry found out yesterday that he may have a crushed disk in his back. The doctor took some X-rays and had him get an MRI last evening. We're waiting to hear back from the doctor as to what the next step will be, but Gerry continues to be in terrible physical pain.

My legs are easing up – mostly because I've done a lot of butt-sitting for the past few days, and that's a mercy, but I just feel so overwhelmed with the work I need to get done.

But our greatest pain today is that our dear, beloved cat Butkis was killed this afternoon. He was hit by a car in front of our house, Hannah saw him first, which is so dreadful. Gerry absolutely adored that cat. Butkis was very special.

I found his mom, a stray, when I lived in Brooklyn. Gerry actually met Butkis first; I was in North Carolina and Gerry was "on call" at the kitty maternity ward in my closet. When the five kittens were born he called my hotel and left the following message at the front desk, "It's a boy! It's a girl! It's a boy! It's a girl! It's a boy!"

As each of the kittens grew older and started to jump out of the big cardboard box they called home, Butkis would sit next to them and blindside them, tackling them (á la Dick Butkus) to keep them in the box. Hence the name Butkis – which should have been Butkus – oh, well...

FEBRUARY TWENTY-EIGHTH
THE BEST THING ABOUT A BLOG
ST. PAUL, MN

... is that one has a 24-hour community with whom to share pain and joy.

Last night was hard. Gerry was up a lot with Gigi, our other cat, both of them mourning. Butkis was really *Gerry's* cat. How odd to feed just one cat this morning.

March

March First
All Home Safe
St. Paul, MN

Max was the last to arrive home on this snowy day, and now we're all in for the evening. We're taking bets on whether there will be school tomorrow.

We miss Butkis so much. Gigi misses him terribly and Atticus, our dog, keeps looking for him around the house.

Gerry's back continues to be a concern. Apparently he has very brittle bones, and Monday they want him to go for a bone density test. He's been told by several folks now that they never (seldom?) see this in someone so young, and in a *man* to boot.

He says it's because he's become a house-husband. Who knows...?

At any rate, I can tell he's concerned – I am, too – but more than anything else is the wrenching pain that envelopes him at all hours. He didn't ask the doctor for any pain stuff, which I partly admire and definitely regret.

I don't want him running around doped up, both of us have substance abuse in our families (we're on the wary side) but he's really hurting.

I finished two crocheted pieces for a book and took notes on them before I sent them off to the publisher, then I shoveled the walkway in front of the house and dug out our car.

I finally tackled Max's bedroom and his loft bed is sleep-able again. Max has a flair for assembling IKEA items. Last night he put together one of the our bedside tables. Gerry put the other together today. It took him about twice as long as Max, but he was working entirely on his knees and resting his back a LOT.

In the midst of all of this work, I don't know WHAT I'd do without Hannah. She's such an incredibly helpful girl, she so much wants to get our house as homey as possible, and I find myself depending on her quite a bit.

March Tenth
Lessons Learned in
Atlanta

Atlanta, GA

This morning I fly back to St. Paul and I'm so excited to see Gerry and the kids. It's been very nice to be back in Atlanta, but I feel like I've hardly left this Gwinnet Center complex for three days.

Here are some things I've learned while in Atlanta this time around:

- Folks in Atlanta are very nice.
- Folks here are also terrific knitters.
- Drivers here are a little – well – *distracted.*
- Tiredness has a way of catching up.
- Lugging the <u>Men Who Knit</u> trunk show up and down hills with no sidewalk sucks.
- iPod makes traveling better.
- I love biscuits.
- It's hard to teach in low light.
- Gerry officially has Osteoporosis.

Risk Factors for Osteoporosis which don't apply to Gerry include: *Being female, Advanced age, A family history of osteoporosis, Being past menopause, Abnormal absence of menstrual periods, Anorexia or bulimia, A diet low in calcium, Long-term use of corticosteroids or anticonvulsants, Lack of exercise, Smoking, Excessive use of alcohol.*

His doctor feels that vertebroplasty is the best treatment. We're both nervous.

March Twelfth
Making It Work
St. Paul, MN

It's amazing how quickly things can happen. Just last Thursday Gerry saw the Interventional Radiologist *(we half expected the waiting room to be filled with family and friends telling Gerry he had hit rock bottom),* and the actual procedure is scheduled for this Wednesday morning.

I told Gerry we shouldn't tell the kids exactly what it entails until after it's over. It's the kind of thing that

Hannah will worry over, and after hearing about her distraction in school from her teacher, she doesn't NEED any new worries. *I'll do the worrying for all of us, thankyouverymuch.*

I only run through my worries like this when my energy level isn't high enough to give myself a good, solid "snap out of it" slap.

Project Runway just announced dates for their casting call. The closest call to me will be in Chicago on April 3rd, so I have a scant few weeks to get the sewing machine out and stitch like a madwoman. (Maybe I can get the gown I designed and knit that my friend Ami wore at the Emmy awards last year...) *Note: Pattern to knit the dress can be found at the back of this book.*

Probably just as vital would be my portfolio, I have to go dust that off somewhere. After so many months of threatening to audition, it would be craven of me to back out now.

March Fourteenth
Wait & See

St. Paul, MN

Gerry's procedure seemed to go pretty well, he was up and walking around a few hours afterward. Now we're home, he's resting, and we'll see in the next few days whether it's had any impact on his pain. We certainly hope so.

It's so odd to face this, as minor as it is *(I know, pain is NEVER minor),* what we both have to realize is that Gerry will probably never be the lifting and carrying guy he's always been. Selfishly, I'm thinking about how it affects me, but *Gerry's* the one with the pain.

After Gerry was settled in with an IV, they directed me to a special surgical family room, divided into cubicles, well-lit with comfortable-yet-slightly-corporate furniture. Some of the cubicles had recliners, some had toys for children.

One had to be "on the list" to get in. *Very velvet-rope, but no bouncer.* What a humane gesture, to create a peaceful space for families who will have an hours-long wait. I watched a bit of Nurse Betty on TV. *(I wondered if it's run on an endless loop on the hospital channel?)*

Did I mention the Valet parking? The $3 Valet parking? The $3 Valet parking which is FREE when they validate the card? *Coming from Jersey, this is very impressive.*

I'm still seething that the back specialist in NJ didn't catch this, and even had Gerry do a few weeks of Physical Therapy before we moved out here. Apparently the PT did NOT help his back.

I did a LOT of knitting while waiting. You knit much faster in a hospital. *(A new slogan for Addi Turbo needles!)*

I wish I had the presence of mind to bring extra needles and balls of yarn, I could tell that several other folks might have benefited from impromptu knitting lessons.

MARCH EIGHTEENTH
WELCOMED!
ST. PAUL, MN

I had the most enjoyable and welcoming evening on Friday at The Yarnery on Grand Street! I can't remember ever living this close to a yarn shop – and what a yarn shop!

So far Gerry's not feeling a lot of relief from his procedure. I can tell that he is a little better from his demeanor, from the way that he's moving easier and the fact that he's just doing more. But when I ask him how he feels, he says that his back is about the same. I can tell he's very disappointed. We're both still waiting, but he was hopeful for a more immediate end to the pain.

This whole Project Runway dream may be coming at a bad time. I was talking with Gerry this week about not doing the audition because of his ongoing health concerns.

He says to go ahead, audition, and if the absolute outside possibility comes true and we have to consider the maniac show schedule, then we'll cross that bridge when we come to it. I'm grateful that he's supportive – but the most important thing is family health.

March Twenty-Second
Sew Busy
St. Paul, MN

I'm working up my three samples for the Project Runway audition, and in addition to the hand knit evening gown I've decided to bring an entirely sewn dress because I don't want them to think that I only knit.

The skirt and back are a sheer woven stripe and the bust area is dupioni silk. I pleated the back along the stripes, and gathered the front just below the bust.

I started yesterday morning, cut, sewed, basted and gathered, then spent the evening sewing. Another few hours finishing this morning, and now the dress is done. *Voila*!

I leave tomorrow for my three-city trip, so I have another day to get stuff arranged for Gerry before I go. More than his back pain, now I worry about his boredom. He's getting sad, he's in pain and he doesn't have a lot to do.

And he doesn't have knitting. Damn. I've tried to teach him in the past, maybe I'll have more success now? *Or maybe it will make him feel like an invalid?*

He's at that point in bad health when you think you'll NEVER get better, and just getting out of bed seems like a huge deal. I'm glad he's resting, though, it's VERY good for his back to just let it relax, he tends to do too much when he's up.

Being out of commission in a new town is really rough – I can tell that Gerry misses his family, too.

MARCH TWENTY-THIRD
PEACE SEEKING MISSILE
MADISON, WI

I feel like I'm busier than I've been in a long, long time, but most of the busyness is just the work of keeping the house going, unpacking, moving in, getting settled. The knitting business is taking a back seat. I guess this is how it "should" be, how it usually is for folks, except the knitting business is also the *mortgage*-earning business. Life throws us curve balls.

And, as silly as it seems, I also feel tremendously *guilty* that I'm not able to do it all. I think guilt is non-productive, useless, absolutely no good to anyone. Yet here I am feeling that I'm not doing enough.

And, of course, that kind of thinking just leads to wheel spinning, and not the fun kind where you make yarn, either! *(I'm watching Rome on HBO and I notice that one of the women seems to be using a spinning wheel. Wha? Her dad just beat her up, probably for time traveling to the 13th century.)*

I'm in Madison, WI, but I wasn't aware they were having the festival of one-way streets this week. *(Apparently I've been crowned the one-way princess! Kneel before my lane shifting prowess!)*

On the way, I stopped at a Wendy's for a chicken sandwich and the girl at the window said, *"Wow – my grandma has the same car! Or maybe it's my great-grandma – one of them..."* Lovely.

God forbid I tell her I knit for a living. I'm 46. Sheesh, when my mom was my age she had a three-year-old daughter *(me)*. Evidently we breed late in our family. But grandmothers tend to be young here.

I'm staying at a lovely hotel, the Madison Concourse. I was upgraded because they're full, so I got to go to the *Governor's Closet* or the *Governor's Suite* or something like that on the 12th floor for some free appetizers and drinks. They'd run out of appetizers, but there was *lots* of gin and tonic.

While I drank I wandered over to the business center on the same floor and printed out some stuff, and called Gerry. *("There's a computer in the BAR?" he asked.)*

While on the computer a gaggle of half-fried businessmen staggered past and one asked me archly, *"Looking at PORN?"*

33

Oh, if only they knew. Knitter's porn – checking out luxury fibers and expensive knitting needles.

Another guy peered over my shoulder and joked to his friends, *"Hey, she IS! This guy has the biggest –"*

– crochet hook.

Worry follows me like that bowl of *Cream of Wheat* that used to hover over the kids on the 1960s television ads. *If you're over 40 you know what I mean, raise your feeble, arthritic hands (if you can).* Worry and guilt, two of the most useless things in the world.

Hannah REALLY misses me when I'm away these days, and I miss her, too. She's at that rough pre-teen age when she knows she's being irritating, but needs continual reinforcement that even if she *IS* irritating, I love her just as much as ever. Which I do. I remember that age so well – it's a hard time. *I think it finally ended last week for me.*

So here I am in my peaceful hotel room, trying to enjoy my solitude and wishing like all get-out that the kids and Gerry were here making a racket.

MARCH TWENTY SIXTH
GRANDFATHER, HEIDI CAN KNIT!
NEW GLARUS, WI

I'm in Swiss Purgatory.

The walls of the hotel are painted with [bad] murals of Peter, Clara and Heidi. Lots of mountains, goats and there's a huge hole in the ice machine. Must have been an avalanche.

I can't get internet reception unless I go downstairs to the business center. (You can tell it's the business center because there's a xeroxed sign on the door which reads,

"Business Center" with clip art of a 1950's business-man.) There's a computer, a lamp and a printer. *Biz-ness? Biz-YES!*

For some reason — evidently known only to Swiss Businessmen — loud yodeling is piped from the speaker in the ceiling. *(Perhaps these are former guests or businessmen, trapped in the 4th level of hell? The yodeling level?)*

My personal theory is that the music is to prevent folks from overstaying the 20 minute limit. It works.

MARCH TWENTY-NINTH
BACK TO OHIO
CLEVELAND, OH

And I'm not even that far from Cuyahoga Falls!

I love Cleveland. I lived here briefly during an internship with the Great Lakes Theater Festival during my last year in grad school, and, ironically, two of my best friends are from Cleveland. Must be something in the water... *(Of course, the water is Lake Erie, so there could be ANYTHING in the water.)*

And how thoughtful of the hotel to put me in a room overlooking the physical plant. It reminds me of my hometown!

I *wish* I had warm, fuzzy memories of Toledo, but leaving it was the best thing I ever did. I'm sure others have much nicer experiences in the town, but when I was a teen, Toledo was known for having the highest suicide rate for kids under 18.

I think of my first 16 years as being a long, long depression with a few light moments of relief.

Toledo was a place where there just wasn't anything to DO except hang out at the mall (and that was even *more* depressing than hiding in my room, singing along to every original cast album I could get my hands on).

Because of my family's deteriorating financial situation as I entered adolescence, we moved from one ugly, depressing house to the next even *uglier,* even *more* depressing apartment. So when I pulled back the curtain on my room and saw the office-park landscape, I felt like I was – *back home.*

On the whole, I'd rather be in St. Paul.

I'm worried about Gerry. Worried enough that I'm considering foregoing the Project Runway audition if he's not in good shape when I get home on Sunday night. He's lost a LOT of weight in the past two months, his clothes are hanging off of him and I can tell he feels like crap. I can also tell that Hannah's feeling the strain. I should be there.

The good news is that after the Project Runway audition I'll be home for a full month, then away for a few days, then home for SEVERAL months. Traveling for a living isn't ideal, but my work allows me a great deal of flexibility to be where I need to be when I'm home. It's the time away that's so hard on everyone.

There is a good chance that when he finally gets in to see the endocrinologist we'll be able to do something for the osteoporosis, which is causing him so much pain and grief. Would he feel good enough for me to go off for the month or so I'd need to be away for Project Runway? I have no idea.

Our St. Paul adventure was my idea – I sort of dragged the family – and now every few days I'm leaving Gerry home alone to deal with everything. Although I love my job I may have to rethink what it is I do for a living. I love to teach, I like meeting so many knitters, I love the designing, but it's a buttload of work for every dollar that I sock away, and means a lot of time on the road.

That's part of my desire to do Project Runway. Yes, it would be a blast, it would be fun and cool and I'm a ham, I can't deny any of that. But I would love to design a line of hand knits for an established fashion company. Could it happen? Who knows... The visibility would definitely help. Oh, did I mention I'll miss the first evening of Pesach by going to Chicago? Please, may I have some more guilt with my *tsimmis*?

I just heard a story on TV about a fire department in Toledo where all the fire fighters had to move into trailers because there's mold at the fire house – *'nuff said?*

March Thirty First
SURROGATE SISTERS
Cleveland, OH

What an unusual and wonderful few days I've had – totally unexpected, and full of love. I'd been pining for some female companionship – missing my friends back in NJ, laughing with buddies while knitting (not being "the teacher"), and I feel the need for a woman's touch in my life.

I called my cousin Jan last week to chat, but had to leave a message. Life is so busy, time is so short, and reaching out to the new friends I've made in St. Paul is difficult when I travel. I hadn't been dwelling on it, but I had a nagging sense that I'd just like to sit and talk with some women friends. Odd how we need that so much. I can only imagine how much Gerry must be longing for a male buddy.

So imagine my surprise when I set up my class materials, turned around to face the class and saw my cousin Jan and her friend, Theresa. What a shock! Needless to say I bawled like a baby. Grandma always told us that we could cry easier than we could piss.

The class was great, it was full *(36!)* and the fact that my cousin – not really a knitter – drove so far to see me was an exceptional gift. It's funny how much it means to me when folks involved in my life in a non-knitting way cross over to the dark side and attend one of my classes or lectures. *Join us...*

Sunday, after all the classes and book signings were finished, Stephanie Pearl McPhee, Lily Chin, Shannon Okey and I went off for dinner. We laughed and laughed, and once again the company of women was a balm to my soul.

On the way to the restaurant we passed a mural of Switzerland, so we all had to leap out of the car and pose in front of it. *(Well, Steph and I posed, Lily smoked a cigarette and Shannon took the picture. We were like girls let loose from school for an afternoon. Lily was the cool one.)*

I love my classes, I love meeting students, but I feel a responsibility to be *"on"* to present myself in a professional way when I'm with folks who are part of a class. This weekend was filled with so many moments when I didn't have to be anything but Annie.

Silly, lost Annie. That felt *very* good.

Shannon Okey & I star in a
two woman production of Heidi.

Photo by Stephanie Pearl McPhee

April

April Third
I Didn't Make It Work.
Chicago, IL

I'm sad, but feeling fine and realistic. A six-hour drive home is a great mind-clearer.

My friend Tom went with me this morning to the audition. He waited outside for a bit until he had to go to work. *(When he left the woman behind me told me that my "husband" was a babe. If she only knew...)* All went pretty well, we got rained on, no big deal. Once inside there was time to steam some of my pieces so they'd look nicer.

Interview #1 was with a 20-something guy who had NO interest in talking to me at all. The young, pretty girls in my group got lots of chat time. Me? He hardly waited to hear me finish my name. *I guess I should have figured the gig was up then.*

The next interview was with a 20-something woman who leafed through my portfolio and said there wasn't enough sewing. I explained that every sweater IS sewn, that the general rules of construction apply to all garments, and that the dress that I brought demonstrated that I was able to sew well. No soap. So I didn't even get past the portfolio review.

I did notice that two pretty-and-hip-young-things in my group were able to forego the portfolio review *(hmmm...)*

I think it was a combination of ME not being visually compelling *(is that a nice way to say fat?)* and the girl who reviewed my portfolio not understanding about sewing/construction/knitting (in other words, she had a bias against knitting...) and, well, both things can be addressed, but not in one day. Too bad.

But I'm home, and I can concentrate on some things that NEED concentrating on. Gerry has an MRI tomorrow, his bone density is rotten and he has high calcium levels in his blood so the doctor's thinking some kind of thyroid thing. This is where I need to be. And Project Runway is out of my system for this year.

In all honesty, this is probably the best outcome; I got to go through with the audition, I know what I need to change if I want to do it next year *(add a few more sewn pieces, lose a few pounds...)* and my heart wasn't 100% in it. I kept thinking, *"This is NOT the time for me to do something like this..."* But I figured that if the one-in-a-million chance happened and I was moved to the next level, I'd deal with that then!

This won't be my year for Project Runway, but maybe next year... Carry on!

APRIL FIFTH

FATE'S WAY

ST. PAUL, MN

Waiting is crummy. Waiting for tests to be done on a family member, is even harder. Gerry has an appointment with a Hematologist next Wednesday, other tests to be done this week. So far no official diagnosis, but the words "Myeloma" and "Multiple" have been mentioned together in the same sentence.

What the frig is *Multiple Myeloma?* I've never heard of it.

Gerry's so pale, he just feels like crap, and I can't do anything to make it better. Well, actually, what I can do is work my butt off so that the mortgage is not a worry on top of all of this. Thank heaven I have two big projects for *Vogue Knitting* to work up between the medical paperwork, taxes and general business nonsense.

And thank heaven the kids are back in school next week!

April Sixth

...And now back to our previously scheduled unpacking

St. Paul, MN

I found an exquisite file cabinet at Target. Our game plan for dealing with this recovery process involves filing information so it's easily accessible. *(And it IS a recovery process, right?)*

I'm sure I've mentioned I'm a Virgo. This is how we deal with STUFF; organize it. That always makes it better, right?

An old college roommate and exquisitely beautiful person sent flowers to help me get over the Project-Runway-doesn't-love-me blues. What a lovely way to know we're in someone's thoughts.

Today Gerry had another test, which wasn't as unpleasant as we both feared, but he has tremendous pain from his hip and we both think there's something going on there.

Have I mentioned Gerry's ulcerative colitis that decided to rear its ugly head? With his continuous back and bone pain he can't get up or down the stairs quickly, so not having a bathroom on the ground floor forces Gerry to spend most of his time upstairs.

And that's just not good for his morale. And his colitis forces me to spend a lot of time in the basement with our badly working new washing machine. *Definitely not good for my morale.*

April Eighth

Eggs, Matzoh, Sunshine & Lollipops

St. Paul, MN

I talked with a good friend yesterday who – before she knew our current situation – broke the news to me that someone very close to her had recently died of Multiple Myeloma. It was quite sudden.

What a coincidence. Life is so odd, huh? Her friend was much older than Gerry *(48 is young to have MM)* and when I explained our situation she was SO apologetic, explaining that if she'd known she wouldn't have been so frank. I was grateful for the frankness.

When folks are unaware someone is facing a specific life hurdle, they tend to be more honest. Honesty is good. However, once they know that they're dealing with a friend in an – *altered* – situation, they tend to be too upbeat. *(Guess what? We can tell you're faking it.)*

I totally understand, and I'm the same way. We want to put a positive, you-can-beat-this spin on a bad situation. I appreciated her unintended cold splash of honesty, though.

I pondered this dilemma this morning *(in our basement shower, brrr)*; how rarely you run into the middle ground. When confronted with a medical discussion, folks are either filled with *Sturm und Drang*, or passing out Sunshine & Lollipops.

And then my mind took a vacation and I imagined the Valkyries singing "Sunshine & Lollipops." Rinse, repeat.

I came upstairs to find a bereft little boy who was expecting Easter baskets to be in front of his door, as they usually are. *Damn that lazy bunny.*

At least I had the wherewithal to BUY Easter treats, but I totally forgot to take them out of the bin in the kitchen and place them in front of his bedroom door. Oy.

So while he "looked" downstairs in the basement for treats, I hid them upstairs. Soon they'll be found, and then the kids will be sated with chocolate and sugar.

We're a multi-faith family; Christian, Jewish, and just pagan enough for a chocolate orgy.

It's becoming painfully obvious that we really DO need to add a bathroom on the ground floor, otherwise Gerry will be relegated to spending 90% of his time upstairs. So we've met with a contractor, the next step is to rough out how we'd like to lay out the alteration and then make a trip to Home Depot to look at cabinets, etc. Our dream is to be able to have the washer/dryer upstairs in the bathroom.

Believe, me, I know it's <u>not</u> the time to start on this. But we may as well get ideas down now. Gerry's tired of being forced to live upstairs, and planning gives me a break in my knitting.

APRIL ELEVENTH
SORTING THROUGH TREATMENT
ST. PAUL, MN

We were in a room today where everyone had a very personal connection with cancer in one way or another – astounding. Not that it should come as a shock, given my own recent family history with the disease, but this was such a hoppin' scene!

So we met yet another doctor, who agrees with all of the previous doctors but – *guess what?* – more tests! So the last three days of this week will be taken up with various tests where they take bits and pieces out of Gerry and look at them under a microscope. He doesn't have a heck of a lot of anything to give up – he's lost about 40 pounds in the past two months and is shorter, too.

My incredible shrinking husband.

This afternoon he said, *"I don't want to fight off a spider with a needle!"*

Gerry's been worried about his pain meds again, this time because he read that they can be bad on kidney function. Thankfully the doc today told him to *please* go back to the pain pills (and even offered Oxicontin, which Gerry turned down. He's afraid of being so dopey that he would fall and break something else!).

We spent the afternoon creating a database of Gerry's medical stuff and sorting out the piles of paperwork we've already acquired. We're finding that this is helping both of us wrap our minds around MM.

The doc would like to start Gerry on Zometa as soon as possible to reduce the calcium in his blood (which is leading to tiredness and confusion) and, as it's a treatment for Multiple Myeloma, he feels that he'd put Gerry on it eventually so he rather do it sooner than later.

For me all of this doctor activity means a lot of late-night knitting – catching up on what I haven't been able to do while driving around from testing facility to testing facility. Thankfully, knitting is the PERFECT activity while waiting for Gerry to get poked *(we each have our needle therapy)*, so I can "go to work" while being the supportive spouse I'd like to be.

Tomorrow off for a bone marrow biopsy. This will help seal the official diagnosis of MM, which all of the docs so far seem to feel is prime suspect. *Where is Helen Mirren when you need her?*

According to Gerry's osteoporosis report he's *"grossly normal."* We're astounded that ANYONE in our family is considered *normal*.

April Twelfth
Celtic Fest at the Oncology Wing
St. Paul, MN

Today we ventured over to St. Joseph's Hospital here in St. Paul for a bone marrow biopsy. We've been there a lot lately, and they're unfailingly kind and thoughtful *(valet parking!)*. According to Gerry, it was about as painful as you'd expect.

He said he couldn't decide whether knowing it was coming made it more or less painful, but the doctor asked me to wait outside while they took a sample from the bones in both of Gerry's hips. His hips and ribs have been the source of a lot of pain, so it may be that there resides a myeloma pocket. Poor Gerry. Moving around hurts; his ribs ache, his hips are sore.

But we're still waiting for the *official* diagnosis. I sat with some nice guys who were getting their chemo and we talked about motorcycles, dogs, politics and knitting. While we were chatting a musician showed up and played a harp, I sat knitting. We presented a very homey picture of life in 19th-century Ireland *(in a chemo ward)*.

Just sitting and talking to folks felt good, and I was sorry that Gerry wasn't able to shoot the breeze with these guys after his procedure. But he was pretty dopey and in pain, so we got home as soon as we could. I did get a lot of knitting done today, my *VK* project's almost finished. I wrote up the pattern this evening, and I'm ready to dive more firmly into a new project tomorrow at the hospital.

They really do try to make the experience as low-stress as possible, and we appreciated it! But stress is definitely stalking us. It's still too chilly to spend much time outside, which would be a nice stress reliever. The stress is making me want to eat a LOT, every pound that Gerry has lost is firmly planted around my middle. To prepare for the battle ahead, I'd like to get down to my fighting weight *(and I don't mean Sumo...)*.

APRIL THIRTEENTH
P.T. THERAPY
ST. PAUL, MN

Gerry's bone scan was pretty quick. He asked for a wheelchair – highly unusual – but I'm glad that he's willing to accept the help. It was SO lovely here today, sunny and warmer, with a promise of even warmer weather this weekend. No word on what they discovered in the scan, and we're not scheduled to see the oncologist again until Friday (the soonest we could get in, he's a busy guy with a *very* full waiting room) so we wait.

I knit in waiting rooms, I thrill and amaze the nurses, and Gerry suffers. Without my yarn and needles, sometimes a crochet hook, I'd be stark raving mad. There is something so soothing in the constant rhythm of my work that helps both Gerry and me put our lives on autopilot and not fret too much as we wait.

One day, long ago, while in line at a post office, I realized that waiting is hard, but the folks who are visibly irritated and impatient make waiting even *harder*.

So we try to be calm as we wait, hoping that we'll make the time pass more quickly for us and for those around us. *How I wish more folks would take up knitting.*

When I'm very stressed I go for drives so I can bawl in the PT Cruiser alone, without scaring the kids or depressing Gerry. I took a drive to Uline Shipping Supply Warehouse here in St. Paul to pick up some boxes and tape, then off to the hardware store for some welding rings for my *Vogue Knitting* project. *Oooh, that sounds either very scary or very cool.*

I let my Dutch side go nuts today and took all the storm windows down and washed the windows. I currently have about half of the screens up, the kids will help me do the rest of them tomorrow. These are the old fashioned kind that swing from the top of the window outside the house and then lock in place with a little lever mechanism. Once I got the hang of it, it wasn't hard. *(The hardest part was how heavy the windows are — that old glass is thick!)*

When I think of how, in other years, I have relied on Gerry to do stuff like this I'm a bit ashamed of my "helplessness" and proud of my current ability to just get done what needs to be done. *I must be eating my Powdermilk biscuits.*

A friend dropped off a book explaining how to open up a window to fix the sash rope, and I'm going to give it a good college try this weekend on two of our front windows. I bought the cutest little crowbar for the job along with the welding rings. *The crowbar will not be in the Vogue Knitting project.*

Tomorrow I'll shop for a shed. I need a place to put these darned windows and I just can't stand the thought of losing that much garage space! Besides, we'll need a place to put the fine push-mower that we're going to buy (we have a small yard, no need for a power mower).

Hannah bought seeds while we were at the hardware store, Blue Delphinium and Cupid's Dart. I have the original brown thumb, but my father's mother was an amazing gardener, and Gerry's mom keeps a lovely garden, so perhaps Hannah's inherited some skill that passed me by? *Cooking and gardening are the homey skills that I haven't seemed to have inherited.*

Everything is so painful for Gerry, but I want him to see the kids discovering and enjoying the Twin Cities this Spring.

I may want too much.

APRIL FIFTEENTH
SAVING BIG MONEY
ST. PAUL, MN

We needed some window washing stuff and other sundries, so I drove on over to Menards for a stroll through aisle after well-organized aisle. I adore hardware stores. I feel like I had a religious experience this morning, I didn't want to leave.

I bought one of those Rubbermaid sheds, which came in two HUGE and heavy boxes, and some brown composite wicker furniture. All of this led to the inevitable rental of the truck, *($20 for 1-1/2 hour)* with lots of help to get my stuff into it.

One guy who helped me was very cute – and a KNITTER! He said he taught himself and I encouraged him to drop by the Yarnover on Saturday *(we'll see...).*

It took me more than the estimated 50 minutes *(yeah, right...)* to put the shed together, more like 2 hours. Then I set up the outdoor furniture, finished washing the windows, put a turkey breast in the oven and hosed down the screens so they're ready to put up.

All of this physical work feels very good. It's tiring, but it's necessary for me right now, mentally, to put my body 100% into hard labor. On Saturday I set up our office upstairs and Gerry handled the computer setup – teamwork!

He's feeling very tired, very beat up *(especially his stomach – the colitis will not abate),* but overall his spirits are good. In most part this is because he's taking his pain meds, and the doctor phoned in a prescription for an anti-nausea drug. He actually ate dinner last night and had a good night's sleep. *Who knew four months ago I'd consider that the sign of a very good day?*

When I called our doctor on Saturday to get something for Gerry's constant nausea, she phoned it into CVS. They called to say they didn't have the drug, but they'd check around for it. They found it at the Walgreens down the street, called and told me, and even gave me directions to get there, very kind.

Tomorrow we have a doctor's visit to our Primary Care Physician to talk about a handicapped sticker for the car and to ask questions about applying for disability. Emotionally this will be a rough visit.

APRIL EIGHTEENTH
HIVE ME
ST. PAUL, MN

Yesterday was a frustratingly, *frighteningly* busy day.

Things I Accomplished:

- *Got Kids up and the house running
  (laundry, dishes, the whole Goya beanery).*
- *Got to listen to Stephanie Miller.
  Yes, this is an accomplishment.*
- *Put together our new Gas Grill that we'd purchased months ago at Target
  (while listening to Stephanie Miller).*
- *Got Gerry to the gastro doc
  for his — ahem — procedure.*
- *Bought a pretty plate at TJ Maxx for $5
  (during the aforementioned procedure).*
- *Finally was able to redeem a credit I've had at Orbitz for a flight to Detroit
  (after almost TWO HOURS on the phone to some off-shore phone bank location).*
- *Got dining room chairs to go with the previously purchased table.*
- *Bought an outdoor rug for our back deck.*
- *Bought a table for the deck*
- *(IKEA as-is, yay!).*
- *Got about 10 rows knitted.*

Things I did NOT Accomplish:

- *I didn't design anything.*
- *I didn't get the disability application finished.*
- *I didn't get the license plates on Gerry's car.*
- *I didn't get to the bank to deposit stuff.*
- *I didn't get Hannah a pair of new shoes.*
  (She's worn through the old ones – a growing girl!)
- *I didn't get a walk in.*
  (Atticus is mad at me)
- *The – ahem – procedure didn't work. Damn.*

And let me tell you, Gerry suffered through not one, but *two* preps. The nurse and I decided that until Gerry's stronger, until the chemo gets going and he gets some strength back, it's senseless to put him through the misery of another colonoscopy.

But he's set on it, he feels it's necessary **now**, so my input may amount to nothing.

Things To Accomplish Today
(or Tomorrow, or Next Week...):

- *All the stuff I didn't get done yesterday, plus...*
- *Find my "shipping box" with my packing list enclosed labels, (I need these!)*
- *Get the flip books delivered, (They're coming today, all 1,300 pounds of them – yikes!)*
- *Get the flip books packaged and shipped.*
- *Get wire. (The wire I ordered was sent to NJ, my fault entirely, so I need to get some stopgap wire for the classes I'm teaching this weekend)*
- *Get my handouts printed. (Much easier now that Gerry's connected our printer to the network so I can print from the living room – yehaw!)*
- *Put aforementioned dining room chairs together (with Max's help!)*

The rest will wait. Life is about prioritizing and dealing with the crappy days gracefully.

April Nineteenth
Eminem
St. Paul, MN

In a roundabout way we got the diagnosis. Gerry's oncologist faxed a copy of a letter for his insurance company with the diagnosis spelled out.

Yes, it is Multiple Myeloma, and the letter said he'd be out of commission for a year.

One year? From what we've read, this sounds like amazingly good news. We'll wait until we see the doctor tomorrow to get the full scoop, but it was a very hopeful fax.

A year is a fathomable amount of time.

This sounds good.

Too good.

April Twentieth
They're Heee–eeeerrrrre!
St. Paul

Flipknits are here, and they're beautiful *[baby]!*

I'm as proud as an – well, as an author looking at 10,000 copies of her new books!

When the driver from the shipping company dropped off

the HUGE pallet of books, I told him that they were all books. *("You must really like to read, lady!")* When I explained what I did for a living he asked where he could sign up to take a knitting class. Creating a world of knitters, one at a time!

I donated a box of the books to the Minnesota Knitters Guild to hand out at the Yarnover tomorrow. I just want to get a bunch of them into the hands of knitters so I can see the flipping happening. I'm so easily amused. *Maybe I'll have all the knitters do The Wave when I give the key note address tomorrow..?*

Today we saw the oncologist and got the official, in-person diagnosis of Multiple Myeloma. He outlined a treatment plan for the next few months and started Gerry on ThalDex (a cocktail of Thalidomide and Dexamethasone) right away. The next step is Zometa, an intravenous drip, which Gerry's already been taking and which will reduce the calcium in his blood and thus help his energy, strength and – not least – his outlook.

I am so proud of how Gerry keeps his sense of humor, his joy, in the midst of what is a scary, uncomfortable and painful time. When Gerry's strength improves and he's feeling better, it will be time for high dose chemo and stem cell transplant *(the cells will be taken from him, not an outside donor)*.

It seems from the doctor's fax that we're looking at about a year of this before we return to our regularly scheduled lives. And, as I said yesterday, a year is fathomable.

It was a year ago tonight that I taught at my first Minnesota Yarnover, and "met" the Twin Cities. And fell in love.

I'm not sure how much I understand all of this myself. Gerry, one of the smartest folks I know, is a little foggy

55

due to the pain meds and calcium in the blood. So I have to educate myself and get on top of it.

Knowledge is power, we strengthen ourselves.

APRIL TWENTY–SECOND
ONE YEAR
ST. PAUL, MN

I enjoyed giving my key note speech at the Yarnover, I'm such a ham. I get a lot of my personal energy from others, from my in-person interactions. Hearing laughter from an audience is like a boost of vitamin B-12. *And my classes were tremendous fun!*

As with last year, I was totally blown away by the expertise and skill of my students here in Minnesota. That was one of the things that made me realize how much I wanted to move here.

It was a year ago that I started the ball rolling toward our family move. And now, here we are. It's a natural time to reflect on the past 12 months, on the wisdom of our move, and how it will impact our future. I've spent a lot of time pondering this lately, and I keep coming back to the conclusion that overall I'm happy to be here. *I hope the family is as happy as I.*

Yes, we would be more physically comfortable in our old house. It was bigger, had a laundry chute *(never underestimate the importance of gravity),* and I didn't have to duck my head when I went downstairs.

But the chances are good, given Gerry's diagnosis, that we might not have *had* that house for long if we'd stayed in NJ. Given our property taxes and the cost of living, we would most likely have already moved into a cheaper house or apartment.

At least this way we were able to sell and move on our own schedule. We loved our home, but as with any breakup it's nice to leave on your own terms.

Here in Minnesota we may not have physical space, but we have *breathing* room. We have a lower mortgage and better recreational and municipal resources. (Never underestimate the importance of busy, happy kids.) Without realizing it, we were battening down our metaphorical hatches when we moved.

Speaking of blessings, although I'm not an overtly religious person, I appreciate the good thoughts that folks are sending and I am happy to accept good vibes from Vishnu, Jesus, Buddha, Great Aunt Mary and anyone else who is thinking lovingly of us. *Thank you!*

April Twenty-Sixth
A Day of Frustrations, A Weekend of Fun
St. Paul, MN

I failed the Minnesota Written Driving Test.

The test you just finished was

Class D

The total number of questions was 38
The number you answered correctly was 29
Your score for this test was 76%

You have failed this test.

I can retake it tomorrow. Tomorrow is another day. And I'll sleep with the exam booklet. When I told Gerry I failed we had this little exchange:

57

G – I've never failed a test.

A – Shut up.

G – Not a written driving test, at least.

A – Shut UP!

G – No, now that I think of it, I haven't even failed the driving portion of any test.

A – Oh - just shut up. *(And you have cancer. So there.)*

Yesterday I bought two bikes on craigslist.com; a Peugeot for Hannah and a Motobecane for me. Gerry's amused himself for a good part of the afternoon checking out both bikes and discovering what has to be fixed. It's good brain and hand work, it takes some muscle, but it's not lifting anything heavy – perfect!

A dear, dear friend who lives nearby offered us the loan of a walker, which we'll take up. It's the groovy kind with a seat, so ostensibly Gerry could sit in the walker for nice long trips to the park or museum while the kids help him along. If he wants to walk but feels self conscious, one of the kids can always ride along.

It's easy to pooh-pooh the pride angle, how awful it feels to be mistaken for someone older and more feeble than you feel. But keeping a good mental picture is vital to recovery.

This walker straddles the line between really necessary, and sort of groovy (it's metallic green). *Vroom*! I hope he doesn't get pulled over.

April Twenty–Ninth
Home (& Gone Tomorrow)
St. Paul, MN

I'm back in St. Paul. What a beautiful sight, coming into the city from the east on I-94 in the evening, the downtown, St. Peter's Cathedral and the state capital all lit up. I have about nine hours to do some laundry, get some rest, then fly out to Detroit.

My flight is in the morning, I'll get in late afternoon *(changing planes – somewhere...)* and then have dinner with my friend Lisa. It will be SO great to see her again!

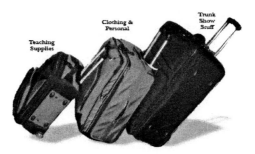

I'll be taping a segment of Needle Arts Studio together with Drew Emborsky on Tuesday – it's good to be so tired, I can't be nervous! Never having been on this show before, I don't know what to expect (but I'm prepared for lots of waiting with LOTS of knitting!). After the show's finished taping I'll drive down to Lambertville to teach at Vintage Yarns.

We used to live one town over from Lambertville, in Temperance, MI *(a suburb of Toledo)*, and it was a hellish period in my life. I had *some* friends, but mostly I was the oddball redheaded kid, butt of all jokes and not able to salvage my self-esteem. That was the year that I became a teen runaway. *(Aka, my Linda Blair period.)*

So back I go – to the scene of the crime – wondering how it will feel to drive around an area where I was so desperately unhappy. I was 14, life was rough. My dad was depressed and self-medicating, I just wanted to be *away*. Being a teen in 1970s Toledo was a hard place to be.

I return home on Wednesday evening and I'm not leaving again until TNNA (The National Needlework Association) in June. Gerry looks good, he says he felt good all day, and he went grocery shopping with the kids. His feet are really swollen, though, so we have to check on that before I leave tomorrow.

MAY

May Fourth
Oncology Marathon
Maplewood, MN

Today turned into an unexpected marathon doctor session – the 9:00 a.m. oncologist visit for Gerry turned into a sudden, *"Let's get a scan of those swollen legs – today!"* so Gerry and I waited around until our appointment at the hospital across the street for his 10 minute scan.

Gerry's feeling better – I can tell he is, but I'm not sure he thinks he is. Which sounds weird. (Wouldn't HE know he's feeling better?)

He's been moving more, getting out a little more, and seems much happier. But when the doctor asked if he felt a difference from the Zometa he said *"No, not really..."* Maybe I'm just seeing what I want to see?

May Seventh
The Last Picture Show
Woodbridge, MN

When Gerry and the kids picked me up from the airport last week we went out to the local Famous Dave's Barbeque joint, and that's when we used the "C" word to describe Gerry's condition to the kids for the first time.

Up until that moment it had been, *"Dad has a blood disease..."* Now that we know a little more about the type of cancer he has, we can speak about it more seriously and honestly.

The kids took it very well. It's good that they have Aunt Jan (breast cancer survivor) and me (pre-cancerous ovarian tumor survivor) as examples of folks who have come through different treatments and are here to tell about it.

So far Gerry and I haven't reached out to the cancer community for support. Just getting through the days is hard enough, it seems there's no time for extra stuff. When we work into a better schedule, we'll be able to reach out to support groups more effectively. Gerry hasn't had a chance to make connections with non-cancer folks in the Twin Cities yet, let alone other cancer patients. I feel like the conduit to the "real world" for Gerry, albeit sometimes a clogged and kinked conduit.

What a shock this has all been – sometimes we just sit and catch our breath. Lots of emotions, lots of change, all at the same time. We're pulling through, though – every day really *is* a gift.

The Ted Koppel special on Discovery last night, "My Cancer," was very informative, hard to watch at times, but necessary. I loved seeing Elizabeth Edwards. I really admire her.

We're finding in this voyage through cancer that one of the tricks seems to be retaining our sense of family and continuing to doing the stuff we like to do together. We like to go out to a cheap dive-esque type of establishment every now and then, it's fun for the kids and a chance to raise them to be cheap dates.

We still go out, but we don't sit in booths (too hard for Gerry) and we time it so that we go when there's no wait – we keep it very short.

Another thing that we love to do as a family is to go to movies. But movie theaters involve too much walking, too many people to wade through, and the seats tend to be uncomfortable for Gerry. This weekend we found a solution just a half hour away; we saw Spiderman 3 at a Drive-In Theater!

It was Gerry and the kids' first time at a drive-in, and a magnificent intro it was! The kids thought it was cool, and loved seeing the movie in the car. Listening to the soundtrack on the radio was an extra kick. A wonderful time was had by all.

Since we were all the way in the back, floodlights were shining through our rear window. It wasn't bright enough to cause a distraction, and it provided me with just enough light to work through a new crochet pattern.

I can see that we'll be doing this again this summer. It's so weird, though, to go to a drive-in and have to contend with all those tall SUV's! *That's a new twist since I was a kid.*

May Ninth
Home Alone
St. Paul, MN

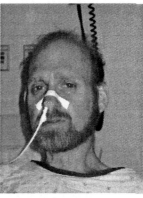

Gerry's not home tonight and I miss him.

This is unusual. I'm the traveler, he's the stay-at-homer (at least he has been the past few years), so it's really odd to be here without him. He's at the hospital.

He went to get a simple colonoscopy and it's been a rough ride. This is try #3. (The first attempt was unsuccessful because he couldn't get the prep stuff down – second attempt failed because he got it down, but it came right back up.)

This time the idea was to pipe it into him. He hadn't realized they meant through a hose in his nose, and it was rough. I dropped him off at 8:00 a.m. and then ran Maxie to school. I was supposed to wait for Gerry to call to have me pick him up, but a little after 11:00 a.m. he called to say they hadn't even started the procedure. Later another call – still waiting – the first attempt at the nose was unsuccessful.

At 5:00 p.m. I called the hospital because I hadn't heard anything and I was worried. All kinds of things go through the mind. But what I found was that after *four* attempts they decided to do a special procedure where they scan his throat while they put the tube down so they have a little guidance.

This attempt *was* successful, but it was too late to actually do the procedure – and they were loathe to let him go home *(worried we'd have a wild, fiber-eating orgy with lots of red Jello, probably...).*

So they admitted him – he's staying there overnight. The kids and I drove over to visit; he was in low spirits. He's pissed that they even had to do this. When his mom had a colonoscopy last month they used a pill prep, no awful liquid, and he's a little angry they just couldn't do that.

They said the pills can cause complications, but he feels that the tube up his nose could cause complications, too.

Poor Gerry – I could tell he felt out of control, angry, just very frustrated. And I was frustrated too. And I felt helpless (the kids were with me and hungry, so I had to take them to get dinner). I feel like I should have been more proactive this evening at the hospital.

I spoke to the nurse about the meds he's on now, what he has to take, and what he has been taking for pain. And although she took notes, she seemed – *vacant* – when she was writing down the information. I don't have a lot of faith that it was processed.

So tomorrow as soon as the kids are off to school I'm off to the hospital to be with Gerry and be more proactive. If I'd stayed with him today, perhaps I could have facilitated the procedure, helped make the whole thing smoother. *Perhaps not.*

MAY ELEVENTH
WHAT A DIFFERENCE A DAY MAKES
ST. PAUL, MN

... we last left our Gerry in hospital, awaiting his colonoscopy.

Well, a tube in the nose and keeping him overnight *still* wasn't enough to – ahem – clean Gerry out sufficiently. So they kept him the rest of the day and gave him *another* 4 liters of the tasty, refreshing Golitely *(...use it as a mixer, or just enjoy it on the rocks!)*

Apparently the 48th time's a charm!

He had the procedure, and everything looks good. Specifically, no polyps, and in an odd twist of fate, it seems the drugs he's being given for the Multiple Myeloma are working wonders on his ulcerative colitis *(aren't you glad you're reading this?)*.

It felt SO good to have Gerry home, and he was glad to be here. This morning when we got up Gerry hit the ground running! I started staining the deck and when I ran out of stain he went and got me more. I didn't want to stop him, because he really *needed* to get out. It was a good outing for him; he stopped and got Chinese Food on the way home. He was desperate for some good Chinese after two days of non-eating.

The deck seems to have come out nicely, staining the banisters took longer than the deck, though. Then Hannah and Gerry put together our new push lawn mower from eBay and mowed the lawn. We all did a little gardening *(pulling weeds, raking, fighting over who got to push the new mower – Gerry lost),* and then a little relaxing on our freshly stained deck.

I am SO happy that Gerry's as pretty inside as he is on the outside. But we have to fatten this guy up!

Tomorrow? We go to the Minnesota Fiber Festival, *aka,* Shepherds Harvest, and we are SO psyched! Gerry will stay at home, I'll take the kids. The bit of walking he did today just about did him in, but I think he really had to prove to himself that he's in control after two days of feeling so incredibly helpless.

May Seventeenth

1,000

St. Paul

Today is my 1,000th blog post. It doesn't seem possible.

And I've made a decision. It was a rough one, but one that must be made for my sanity. I've been fretting the past two days over knit design submissions to the major magazines, and this time I'm just going to forgo them. I need a bit of a break. I need to work on the stuff I have to do for ME (work-related *and* family-related), and I need to recharge my batteries. If only I didn't feel the amazing guilt.

The improvement since Gerry's colonoscopy is amazing. I'm sure a large part of it is the medication he's on. It's also clear how good he feels to be home. But most of all, I think he had this fear that there was something going on down there. Both his mother and father had colon cancer (as did my mom – not that that has any impact on Gerry's health, but it plants the whole CC thing firmly into both our minds).

So the positive news from the scope was a real relief, and I think it shows in Gerry's general health. He's more mobile than he's been in *months*, he's still walking – with difficulty – but he *insists* on going shopping.

He runs errands and he may even go with me to watch the kids taking their tennis lesson. I signed Maxie up for baseball and I don't know who's more excited, Max or Gerry!

Another thing that's greatly increased Gerry's mobility is the handicapped tag we now have. Avoiding those extra 200 yards of walking to a store makes him much more willing to get out and about. And, once I brought home that borrowed walker, he seemed to want to prove that he does *not* need it, so I guess it worked.

Things we've planted are starting to grow. Hydrangeas are taking root and I planted several rose bushes.

We went to Ikea a few days ago to look at kitchens, we saw some stuff we liked, and then we had dinner. As we were getting our trays and silverware, both kids demanding immediate answers to questions, Gerry asking me questions, all while I'm trying to herd them into line and make sure they take *two* vegetables and *one* dessert.

When it came time for me to order, I was a total blank. *What did I want?* Who knows? I just took the next thing they slid up on the shelf (meatballs and a salad).

It was a minor incident, but seems indicative of my life these days. I feel like the *Answer Woman*, but I have to make sure that I give *myself* the space that's required to find the answers.

I have no idea what I really want for myself. At this point I'd settle for more energy to answer more questions.

Tomorrow we go to the oncologist again for another monthly round of Zometa and to seek some kind of time frame for the stem cell transplant this Summer.

I'd love to be able to send the kids back to South Orange for a week to stay with friends. Several Jersey parents have asked if Hannah and Max would come for a visit – our kids are missed! – and it would also be good to have them away when Gerry starts the high dose chemo. I know chemo's not as bad as it used to be, but calming kids' fears while Gerry's trying to figure out how he'll deal with this new phase may be a difficult juggling act.

When we first decided to move to St. Paul, our grand plan was for Gerry to dive headlong into providing home support for the knit business while I traveled, taught and designed the Spring and Summer away. Well, obviously there was a little *hitch* in that plan, and most of my time has been spent playing catch up with little long-term planning.

When you lose your job, you feel the paycheck ending immediately. When you're a freelancer and you slow your output, it sometimes takes months for the bank account to catch up. It's one of the oddities of freelancing – often when you're working your butt off the bank account is empty, and when you have a dry spell the checks start coming in. We knew that moving out here would be a gamble – losing Gerry's income when he quit his job – but we also figured that my increased productivity would make up for it.

So much for the increased productivity! I'm productive *enough*, we're okay, but I haven't been able to restock the inspirational pantry as quickly as I'd like. Let's just say that I've never been happier that we're a naturally frugal family. I'm feeling relieved that Gerry's finally agreed to go check into Social Security disability benefits.

He's spending a lot of his time getting everything together and surfing the web for information on what exactly will be required of him at the Social Security interview. He was happy to see that Multiple Myeloma was specifically mentioned as a bona fide reason for disability – yay.

Who knew four months ago that this would be a source of happiness?

May Twenty-Sixth
Heart-to-Heart at 6 a.m.
St. Paul, MN

We're meeting with contractors to see about turning our not-very-useful largish kitchen into a more useful kitchen and bathroom. Doing this bathroom addition is a hard thing to swallow, but we budgeted for it when we bought the house. We were lucky when we sold our house and ended up with a small pocket of cash we'd earmarked for a kitchen renovation.

We really need it now, and I know in my heart of hearts that it will dramatically increase our home's value. It's still hard. Having Gerry stay upstairs for much of the time is harder.

We're doing okay, but we had to have an honest talk with ourselves about the money we've socked away for the kitchen, and what this coming year may bring.

Of course, given the past three months, we've begun to eat into it, which is frighteningly easy to do. Right now I have to cut down on teaching engagements in order to be here for medical stuff, for the family and for Gerry. Add to this the fact that half of our wacky kitchen lacks a foundation and we've decided to scale back the renovation so there will be no addition. The main thing is to get a bathroom on the first floor, period.

Gerry woke up this morning wondering if we even *need* a contractor, but I'm thinking with all of the other stuff that we're carrying on our backs, the last thing we need is to act as our own contractor.

I remember having really good, high-energy days when I was recovering from my hysterectomy a few years back. I'd make big plans, assuming that the energy boost was here to stay. But then two days later I'd crash. Tired, barely able to get downstairs, let alone re-seed the back yard or whatever I'd decided I just *had* to do.

It may be that Gerry is feeling a boost of energy now. We've had a good week, a few *really* good days, but still the pain is always present and I can tell he's absolutely exhausted.

Perhaps part of the "no contractor" thinking was due to the pain pill I got him at 4:30 a.m. when he woke up very sore? Who knows? Those pain pills can make you feel like you can do anything. For a few hours.

May Twenty—Ninth
Man Proposes
St. Paul

Today was rough. We met with a doctor and social worker at the University of Minnesota's Bone Marrow Treatment Clinic, they discussed treatment options *(really, only one option),* and their words reinforced what we'd read, but hadn't entirely digested.

Or, as the online Merck Manual says:

> *Because multiple myeloma is ultimately fatal, people with this disease are likely to benefit from discussions of end-of-life care that involve their doctors and appropriate family and friends.*

> *Points for discussion may include advance directives, the use of feeding tubes, and pain relief.*

Suddenly that one year time frame seems a bit more ominous. Silly me, I thought they meant one year until Gerry was back to his old self, not one year, *period.*

I took notes today – I know I did – but when I look at them I find them indecipherable. I need a translator to read my notes. In college when I was failing Zoology, I had the bright idea to take my notes in French – which I was also failing. I ended up almost failing both classes. I could have been reading those notes yesterday.

The doctor we spoke with was very nice but very soft spoken. I wish I could have heard what she was saying better. It seems so inelegant to keep saying, *"Huh?!"* when you're told that the love of your life has terminal, incurable cancer. She did her best, but we definitely had a delayed reaction to her words.

Huh? [beat] *Excuse me?*

I noticed a sign in the elevator explaining that translators would be available for non-English speaking patients and family members. I wonder if I can get a medical-to-English translator?

One thing we definitely *did* understand was the phrase, "*One to Three Years…*"

We both gulped hard – we were very adult – we didn't cry (at that moment) and Gerry was amazing with his stack of test results and envelope of paperwork. Later at home he asked me if he seemed obsessed with his manila envelope. Manila envelope = vague sense of control over MM.

I have a database and a file cabinet. Gerry has a manila envelope. Each of us clings to our own coping mechanism. We're dragging the manila envelope plus every family document we've acquired in our 15 years of marriage down to Social Security tomorrow when we go to convince them that yes, he *is* sick and cannot work.

There's a 6 month waiting period from application date until disability payments begin – *ch' and ching* – so the drunken sailor spending will have to stop. Actually, I'm being facetious. We're spending like very sober sailors. The small extravagances aside, and the line of credit we're taking out to create the bathroom notwithstanding, we're a frugal lot.

Wish us luck tomorrow with the bureaucrats *(another language I never mastered)*. I think I scooted into "dealing with it mode" with alarming speed. *Hmm, maybe THIS is my coping mechanism?* Or perhaps I'm in denial.

But in my heart of hearts I feel that Gerry's going to be in the 10% that makes a good, full, longer-than-five-years recovery. *And you know I'm never wrong about these things.*

I wish we had unlimited money – don't we all? – so I could just take time off and be with Gerry. I'm doing quite a bit of that this summer, but bills are bills. Ours aren't going to stop any time soon. The last thing I want to do is cancel teaching dates, but looking at my Fall teaching schedule I'm getting a little scared about being able to be with Gerry when he needs me.

We were told by the Social Worker at University of Minnesota that now is the time to rely on friends and family in the area.

This is the point I broke down sobbing in the office. *(Not when they told me that the worst case scenario is that Gerry is looking at three to five years. No, I cried because we'll have to ask for help. Lovely.)* And what a helpful thing bursting into tears is – if only I had been alone in the car.

Part of me is happy to be going to TNNA on Thursday. I'll see a lot of friends, teach some classes, and do some schmoozing. Work is good for occupying the obsessive part of the brain.

But another part of me is afraid I won't be able to face *anyone* without bursting into tears. Or vice versa. This has been known to significantly reduce the enjoyment of a class, so I promise not to do that. I can't promise that I won't have a lot of "bathroom time" during the weekend. My own little porcelain, tile and chrome oasis.

I've heard that both weeks of the France trip is sold out. However, Gerry is tentatively scheduled for his transplant in September, so we'll have to make sure they don't overlap. Nice how Gerry's health is planned around my teaching schedule, huh?

I should probably think about renting a car just to have something to sit in and bawl. I think I may be avoiding some of the parties. On the other hand, can you say, *"Open Bar?"*

May Thirtieth
Crying Game
St. Paul, MN

I've just had the worst haircut disaster of my life. I look like a – well – let's just say that folks are going to be

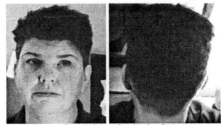

checking the size of my hands. Fabulous.

Evidently there was a breakdown of communication, I just didn't make myself clear. *Yet another translator is needed.* The top is short, the sides and back are even more drastic. That's what Gerry called it, *drastic.*

"It's a – drastic – haircut, hon. But it IS May."

The implication being that by the time September rolls around my summer haircut may be *just* long enough for the customs officials to allow me into France, where I'm going to teach for two weeks. Max told me I looked good (revised to *"not bad"* when I told him to be honest).

I'm knitting a silk headband to wear around my head at TNNA. I'll keep a tally tomorrow as I fly to Columbus how many folks address me as *"Sir..."*

June

June Seventh
Making Peace With My Hair
St. Paul, MN

So I returned to the salon for a *"fix"* and we decided to wait on a color. When I walked in I was a lot more upset than I realized – I also figured out rather quickly that I just wanted someone to say, *"We're so sorry about your hair!"*

Once I made that clear – sometimes asking is the best way – everything was cool and they were very sorry about my hair. We were *all* sorry. And I found the picture that I'd shown the original stylist. (Princess Di on the cover of Bazaar, with a sort of Brideshead Revisited public school boy cut). I *knew* I wasn't insane.

I'm more than willing to take a certain amount of responsibility for the original haircut. I'm thinking of it more as a breakdown in communication than *"They tied me down and forced a bad haircut on me!"* I figure that's one way I can grow from this experience. *Hopefully my hair will grow, too.*

> I said "Princess *Di.*"
> The stylist heard me say "Princess *Dyke...*"

So I had a different stylist this time, and I really wasn't expecting much. But she was able to "texturize" my hair, shorten the top a bit so it wasn't *quite* so Sergeant Carter. And she was able to "round out" my head. Evidently I have a square head.

I feel like it's a whole new haircut, and I'm really much more at peace with it. I can actually LOOK at myself in the mirror without bursting into tears *(and isn't that all any of us want?).*

Today was Field Day at Max's school, so I volunteered at the Oversized Clothing Relay. It was a friggin' *hoot*! I think I got the best assignment of the day. I kept yelling at the 3rd graders as they ran by in gigantic pants and shirts, *a la Joan Rivers, "WHO ARE YOU WEARING?"*

Well, I know *I* enjoyed myself! Tonight – if it doesn't rain – Max has baseball again. Woo!

June Ninth 2007
Knitting The Threads From Which I Hang
St. Paul, MN

Friday Gerry had his monthly Zometa drip – always exciting – they're moving next month's drip up so that he'll have it before the 4th of July.

He hadn't felt very good all week, tired and achy. We think he may be fighting off a cold. At the doctor's office they discovered he had a fever and that he was a bit dehydrated, so in addition to the Zometa they also gave him some fluids intravenously to pep him up a bit. I was struck by how unexpectedly serious such a seemingly *minor* thing would be.

The extra drip was going to take about an hour. The kids would be home from school in 20 minutes, so I drove home to pick them up, then drove back to Maplewood to get Gerry. I finally experienced the joy that is St. Paul rush hour. Twice. *My, you folks DO start your rush hour early out here!*

So many things about this situation are hard. One of the hardest was the heart-to-heart I had with the kids in the car. I remember many difficult conversations about my dad's health with my mom in the forced intimacy of our car, *déjà vu*.

78

We had previously mentioned the word *"Cancer."* Max heard it, but apparently Hannah hadn't and she was surprised to hear it in connection with Gerry's illness. We discussed the kind of cancer Dad has, what the treatment will be, and I danced around the prognosis.

The kids were terribly upset that Gerry may have to be in Rochester, MN for two months. I didn't even go to the *next* place. One step at a time.

This is hard. That seems to be such a self-evident statement, that I feel silly saying it. And – more self-evidence – it's much harder for Gerry than it is for anyone else.

Friend In College Sez:
"Annie Modesitt, Mistress of the Obvious."

Yes, it's hard for me, hard for the kids, but hardest for G. I never want to lose sight of that. It's easy to get very "me" centered – *How does this affect ME?* – but that's a little whiny when the issue is so much more serious for Gerry.

Emotional meltdowns do not make the situation easier for Gerry, which is why I tend to have them far away, usually in the car. I can be a little witchy when I melt down. *"I'm melting!"*

There are a few friends here I can break down in front of here in Minnesota, but not as many as I had back in New Jersey, and I miss them.

It takes time to develop the kind of friendship that allows you to be a slobbering, snotty-nosed, weepy, red-faced lump and not lose your dignity. *Not that I don't do that in my classes, but that's performance art.*

Sadly, yesterday that happened in public (at the public *library*, to be exact...), and I lost control. I hate that. I feel like I'm just hanging by a thread many days, which is not a comfortable position to be in. *It makes me do mad, crazy things like ending sentences with a preposition.*

But there are so many good options, for example a long walk with Atticus, that can quell the impending storm. The seriousness of our situation becomes very real at the oddest moments, sparked by innocent little things that a few months ago would have been a minor annoyance or even a joke.

Now they bear more weight – I bear a lot more weight – and I'm not just talking about how tight my shorts are fitting these days.

> Aunt Lorraine Sez:
> *"Oh, Annett-y, do you always have to act a'fool?"*
> *"Yes. Yes I do. Now get back in the box."*

Yesterday, after trimming the hedges and doing some yard work with Maxie, I took the kids off to Comotown to give Gerry a little rest after his big day. He's been admonished to *keep his feet up* (which he won't do) because the steroids are causing swelling.

We had a great time – they rode the rides and Hannah made an appearance in a magic/comedy show while I knitted a tremendously beautiful piece of fabric from Tilli Tomas yarns. It's going to be a turban, very Norma Desmond. I'm excited about the construction of this piece.

Then we went to the grocery store and stocked up on *stuff*. Always more *stuff*. I lost my cell phone, I found my cell phone (it was in the pocket of my bag, where it belongs, and where I found it after sending Hannah out to the car – then going out there myself).

Have I mentioned my mind is taking little holidays without pre-approved consent? I'm afraid of running out of vacation days.

We dropped off the groceries at home, picked up overdue books and tapes, and off to the library.

Apparently, a few weeks ago while I was away, Max took out 2 movies (*Star Wars* and *Home Alone*), and promptly forgot that he had them. That's our Max. The sweetest boy around, but he has his forgetful moments. Oh, he's nine.

I've been so distracted (overwhelmed?) that things slip past me. On a slow day I contend with getting Gerry to appointments, Max to Baseball, Hannah to wherever, writing, design work, the Social Security interview, digesting the Multiple Myeloma diagnosis and its implications, my teaching...

My Fourth Grade Teacher sez:
"Annette Modesitt, you are an EXCUSE-MAKER."

As I pulled out my wallet to pay the $10 fine on the first DVD, I was hoping to reduce it a bit by explaining our current circumstances. So I explained that my husband had been diagnosed with MM, due dates had slipped past me, *yada, yada*. The clerk dispassionately, and a little distastefully, said, *"That'll be $10."*

I felt hot and cold and my throat went dry. *"Uh oh, I'm on the verge of losing it..."* popped into my head. I asked if there was a manager I could speak with. He gave me a business card and said they'd be in *"maybe tomorrow..."*

Okay, I paid the $10 and glared at my son. *That's 2+ weeks allowance, Max.*

Then the clerk told me about the *other* fine, which totaled $20. I moved toward that dark, rainy, teary place that is usually only experienced in the privacy o^f the PT Cruiser.

I said, *"Look, is there anyone here today I can talk to – any manager on duty? $30 is a lot of cash for fines..."* He directed me to a woman over at the information desk. I told the kids to wait and walked over to her.

I know I looked like a maniac with my red and white face and skull length hair. I waited until she was finished with the woman ahead of me and explained the situation.

Lo and behold, there IS a policy of forgiveness for fines when folks are dealing with this kind of, I'll just say it – shit. *Yay, shit!*

Of course, I was so close to the edge that any kindness was just the tap I needed to fall over the edge. I excused myself and went to the bathroom for a good cry. (Damn! Of course the library has a money-saving, ecologically minded, St. Paul sensible bathroom with the hot air hand dryers and no paper towels.)

I walked back out to where the kids were calmly (thank *heaven*) waiting for me. The on-duty manager approached me to say, in a sympathetic way, *"I know what you're going through – my brother-in-law had that. He just died a few months ago."* I said, *sotto voce, "We're trying not to go there in front of the kids right now..."* I think she got it.

Unfortunately, the kids got it, too – it was a rotten and rough moment. We had a very quiet car ride back home. Then Max and I drove back and returned *Home Alone*. Hannah stayed home so Gerry wouldn't be alone.

I want to go back, I have a book on hold, but I feel way too ashamed of getting so upset while there to return. Maybe I can wear a wig?

The original clerk's attitude is one that I've run into before. Not rude, not unfriendly, but sort of quietly shocked that I would expect to skirt the rules. *Just who do I think I am?*

I am not entirely sure some days.

At times life makes some rules seem pointless.

June Eleventh
People Say The Darndest Things...
St. Paul, MN

Things I'd *really* like to say when folks make nice-but-slightly-thoughtless comments:

– "Everything will be alright!"

Thanks.
(Can I get a signed guarantee on that?)

– "Doctors don't know what they're talking about!"

You're right.
(And your medical degree is from <u>what</u> hospital?)

– "You need to be *positive*!"

I will.
(Are you blind? Can't you see that I am?)

– "Don't lose hope!"

I won't!
(I hope we have a good life – I'm not losing that.)

– "This is part of God's plan..."

– Okay...
(Well, allow me to say the plan sucks. And why is She telling everyone else but us? Hey, stop talking behind our backs!)

What would I really like – no, *need* – folks to say?

This sucks.

You *can* get through this.

Life is *still* beautiful.

Hi.

So – what DOES one get the man who needs more time for Father's Day?

June Twelfth
Okay... So I'll Ask
St. Paul

I have learned the hard way that the asking for help is the most difficult thing to do. But I've also learned that people are so thankful to be asked, given a task, made to feel helpful that they are usually very grateful for the direction.

The social worker at the University of Minnesota told us about www.lotsahelpinghands.com, which coordinates helpers for cancer patients. It looks as though it may work well for us.

We just got the word that the Mayo Clinic can see us tomorrow. As in Wednesday. We're squaring away baby sitting for the kids tomorrow. Hopefully we can make that come together. If worst comes to worst, we can take them with us. *(But I have a feeling this will be another one of "The Talks" and it's best that Dad and Mom have the car ride home to collect themselves before seeing the kids again...)*

Perhaps, more testing on Thursday and Friday (and Saturday?) to determine if/when the stem cell transplant should happen. In case of more testing we'll probably get a hotel room for Gerry so I can return home and be with the kids those nights. If only I could split in two. But I barely have enough hair for one person.

JUNE THIRTEENTH
SEVEN-THREE-OH
ROCHESTER, MN

We heard the news today that we didn't want to hear *(oh boy)*.

Dr. Costas at the Mayo Clinic was frank. He said the time frame we're looking at is a couple of years. He has a strong Brazilian accent, it sounded like he said, *"A cup-full of years —"*

Me: A *cup FULL* of years?
Dr. C: A *couple.*
Me: A *couple?*
Dr. C: A *couple.*
Me: As in *TWO?*

Although Dr. Costas *did* say that sometimes folks with Multiple Myeloma go on for long periods of time, it's not common. He wasn't hopeless or pessimistic, just realistic.

We appreciate this, we've not based our marriage on false hopes, we're pretty honest with each other. It seems this is the best way to continue – hopeful but realistic. Gerry seems as if he hasn't 100% absorbed this. *Sweet Mary, I haven't either. Who could?*

I'm clinging to numbers, things that can be quantified. It was stressed to us that everyone is different, every scenario unique. All they can tell us are the averages.

My mind is filled with more averages and statistics than the sports page.

730 days.

17,520 hours.

24 months.

We've had 15 years together.

Married 8/21/93.

Max is 9 and Hannah is 10.

Gerry was born on Feb 2, 1959.

Useless numbers.

It was a long and quiet ride home. The good news is that Gerry's body is responding well to treatment, although his spirit isn't. The bad news is that even though he's responding well, he's already in stage three Multiple Myeloma.

So our second opinion at Mayo was somewhat worse than the first opinion at University of Minnesota. The three year life expectancy time frame we were given at U of M was reduced to two years at Mayo.

Remember this when you say you want a second opinion.

At the Mayo they are hopeful, but they want to make sure our own expectations are realistic. They promise nothing, and guarantee nothing. *It's life, not a radial tire.*

Dr. C: What are your expectations for this treatment?
Me: A 50th wedding anniversary?

Realistically, though, we're looking for a little hope. And a little more time. *"Hi, we just moved in, I'd like to borrow a 'cup full' of years..."*

We're definitely in the right place, though. Mayo is the hotbed of Multiple Myeloma research. They do 300+

blood and marrow transplants a year. We're in good hands. In spite of all of the crap, I think we still feel very lucky. (Okay, maybe not *very* lucky. But I know we'd rather do this together.)

Heads up everyone – never, *ever* complain about growing old in front of me.

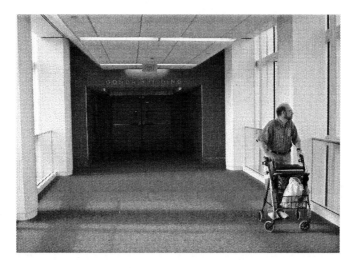

June Fourteenth
Mayo Recap
Rochester, MN

We've had our field trip to the Mayo Clinic in Rochester (twice) and have met with a few people.

Now we wait.

Gerry has a lot of pain, which makes everything much harder. One of the hardest things is convincing him to *take his pain medication*, but slowly we're getting that message through. He's stoic, our Gerry. We just got a scrip for Oxicontin. Heaven help us if he starts spouting Rush-isms...

We're told that he's already in stage three Multiple Myeloma, but these stage things aren't used that much anymore because they're so inexact. Gerry's frustrated because they keep telling him his numbers are good, but he feels like crap.

Gerry and I are not being pessimistic, just realistic. And we are hopeful. This is how we live our lives; frugal, pragmatic and realistic. We have a great marriage and a lot of fun together, but ultimately we see things as they are, and try to deal with them gracefully.

We can't change who we are right now just because it might make it easier to tell folks *"We're positive he's going to be in remission – we refuse to believe otherwise!"* We are who we are. Neither of us has ever been a fan of the "failure is not an option" mindset. Humanity is our only option, and humanity = failure sometimes.

Faking something at this point would just be very sad and not what we love best in each other. This is amazingly hard. I never knew anything could be so hard, and if it's hard for me, I can only imagine how difficult it is for Gerry.

It still doesn't seem to have sunk in fully for either of us. I think we have to take small bites of this big meal to fully comprehend it.

We'll have a brief moment when it will dawn on one of us that Gerry probably won't see Maxie playing ball in high school, may not meet Hannah's first date, won't be there when I finally run for president *(oops, I didn't mean to let that slip...)*.

Small bites. Many, many small bites.

JUNE SIXTEENTH
BACK TO SOME KNITTIN'
ST. PAUL, MN

Yesterday the loveliest thing happened. Friends came by with a bucket from the Colonel, some grapes and carrots, and all the Diet Coke a girl can drink. It's my weakness, Diet Coke. I don't keep it in the house because I'd overdose, but when I'm out of the house I'll have it. My own version of *house kosher.*

And they stayed for a visit. Love the visits. Gerry was feeling really good, he had lunch with us, Maxie had a great playdate with my friend's wonderful son, and I got to sit and chat with friends while we all knitted. It truly was just what the doctor ordered.

Then I received some yarn for a colorwork piece for *Vogue Knitting*. And, wonder of wonders, the photo shoot's been pushed back so I have an extra two weeks. Life is good. You know, in the midst of the deepest crap on the planet, life is good. Even when it sucks, there's a beauty, like the view from our back deck.

89

I did a little shopping for Father's Day, then home to see G sitting on the back deck, enjoying the Wifi and checking email. I was so grateful and happy to be just sitting with my guy on the back porch that I spilled the beans a day early about our big Father's Day Gift.

When the possible date for the stem cell transplant was moved up to August instead of late September, I realized that my pipe dream of taking Gerry with me to Southern France, where I'm teaching in mid-September, was NOT going to work. I also very much wanted to have a family vacation while he's able to enjoy it, and the kids are able to spends some great, quality time with him.

Since I'm teaching up in Duluth next weekend I've checked out rental properties in the area and found a lovely home right on Lake Superior for the five days after my engagement. It will eat up my earnings for the weekend, but it's worth it.

So I jumped the gun and revealed the secret. Gerry's happy, the kids are happy, and Atticus is the happiest because the owners have agreed that he can come.

JUNE TWENTIETH
PAYBACK, BABY...
ST. PAUL, MN

Yesterday I got to pay the universe back a little bit for the myriad times I've been ferried around new towns by kind folks, sometimes in blizzards (but usually just in a car...). [rimshot] *Thank you ladies and gentlemen, I'll be here all week...*

Amy Singer, the founder of online magazine knitty.com – la Knitty, as we call her – was in town to speak at the Minnesota Knitter's Guild and also is teaching a lace class. I volunteered to be her wheels and gave her the

Cook's tour of St. Paul, starting with my home and an intro to Gerry (tired, but in good spirits).

Then we dropped her bags at the hotel and on to a wonderful lunch at Dixie's (there's a TRAIN in the ceiling). Amy snapped a photo of a PT Cruiser for me (there is an inordinate number of them, I've started a photo essay, *"The PTs of StP"*) and we finally headed to Dunn Bros for coffee before arriving at the Textile Center.

The most gratifying part of the day was seeing how much Amy loved St. Paul. I know that I loved this area when I visited last year, I know that my family loves it. But it's so special to have someone new come to town and see all the beauty and earnest, crunchy goodness that I see.

Amy's talk was based on her new book, <u>No Sheep For You</u>, and she was quite informative and entertaining. There is SO much I don't know about fiber, and the talk cleared up a lot for me. I loved her explanation of non-animal fibers, how the fibers are pulled/extruded and finally spun to create non-wool yarn. (My mom used to work at a Viscose factory during the war, so I have a more *personal* relationship with Rayon than Amy does.)

Then I drove Amy back to her hotel and we walked across the street for a late dinner (against the light – for *shame* you Canadian, flaunting our laws like that!). Afterwards I drove home to watch the Colbert Report with my honey.

Today we're going to have coffee with Jennie The Potter because Amy – having exceptional taste – loves Jennie's stuff as much as I do. I may even walk Amy over to Minnehaha Falls *(she thinks I'm joking...)* for a stellar cap on the day.

Did I mention it's sunny and in the 70s? And Atticus is groomed? And Gerry put together a wire shelf in the basement?

All-around good. I worry that he wears himself out *(Gerry, not Atticus)* but I hate to hound him about it.

A fine line between cautious wife and harridan.

JUNE TWENTY-SECOND
NOTHING GOLD CAN STAY
ST. PAUL, MN

We're in a very golden time now, probably the best Gerry will feel until a while after the bone marrow transplant. They've cut down some of his meds so he doesn't have as many side effects, but he still benefits from the Zometa and steroids. I hope he continues to feel this well through July and is in good shape for the transplant process, scheduled to begin on August 7th.

Today we're meeting with a contractor to actually hear the bid on turning our kitchen into a kitchen/bathroom. Then Jennie The Potter is picking me up and we're off to Duluth together. She's doing a craft show up there, I'm speaking to the guild and teaching, then she'll drive home and I'll hang around waiting for Gerry and the kids to arrive on Sunday.

Max hit the ball several times at his game yesterday, and made a play at first base. I was here working on house stuff, so I missed it. Perhaps he only does well when I'm not there...?

At any rate, Gerry was able to go to the game and saw the magnificent play. It meant the world to Max.

JUNE TWENTY-FOURTH
THE DULUTH MISTRESSES
DULUTH, MN

Not to be sexist or anything, but does it bother anyone else that probably 98% of the folks who have completed The Knitting Guild Association (TKGA) Master Knitters Program are women? Myself, I'm waiting until they call it the *Mistress* Knitters Program (or maybe the *Consummate* Knitters Program?). I know that *"mistress"* has a double meaning, but *"master"* isn't exactly free of negative connotation, either...

I had the nicest time at the guild on Friday night, they made me feel so welcomed. Knitters are amazing. Some of the women had been in my classes at the Yarnover; it was nice to see them again. I don't remember *every* person in all my classes, but I'm amazed at how many I actually *do* remember (if not names then small, useless details like their husband was related to Gil Hodges or they own a standard poodle).

I think when we have a passion – whether it be knitting, gardening, fishing or anything else – we share our personality through that passion. We can use the passion to help us shape our world, or to understand parts of life that can be mysterious.

I tend to remember the way folks knit, how they talk about their knitting, whether they're tentative or fearless. It's much easier than remembering their names. I'm afraid this forgetfulness on my part will be seen as rude at times. I do *try* to remember names, but I seldom forget knitting.

The students who came to the classes were a pure delight, and I felt comfortable enough with all of them to berate them mercilessly *(I kid because I love)* and engage

93

in some tough knitting. Best part of the class? When I told them they'd be cabling without a cable needle by the end of the class and they looked at me in total disbelief! I *so* enjoyed that.

And guess what? *Everyone* was cabling like a friggin' Irishwoman by the end of the class! Even the woman who told me that she didn't know how to purl. HA! She just didn't *know* that she knew how to purl!

I have to look at a map at least once a week to remind myself exactly how far north we are, and how that affects the quality of the sunlight. Now I'm sitting at a Dunn Bros Coffee across the street from a water park hotel, waiting for Gerry and the kids to drive up so I can give them all big kisses and hug them until my arms get tired.

When my heart is in such a sensitive state, one day away feels like a week. I worry about the kids being away for so long in New Jersey this summer, but I'm heartened by the fact that they'll be with good friends.

Thank heavens for *love*.

JUNE TWENTY-FIFTH
BLACK EYE
DULUTH, MN

I have a black eye. It actually looks now as though I'm just wearing a lot of eye shadow on my right eye. I like to think of it as my Clockwork Orange look.

I wish I had a really fun story about how I got it, but it was a taxi driver. Specifically, it was a really rude driver who refused to put my bags in his [filthy] cab.

I didn't want them in the trunk with the dirtiest spare tire in history. Putting them in the back seat on the [ripped and torn] upholstery was so far out of his job description that I put them in myself.

As I shoved one of the bags along the seat I hit my eye on the back door. That's the story.

Suffice to say we did *not have a pleasant ride. As he drove off he yelled, "You may THINK you have a pair, but MINE are bigger!"* which I found amusing because he was hugely fat and had man-boobs. He may have been alluding to a different part of his anatomy, but I figured was he was bragging about his bra size.

Oh, and he smelled. Eh, I guess there's one in every town.

So imagine how thrilled I was to see Gerry and the kids arrive at the motel! Always great to see my family – and the dog – and the PT Cruiser – all in one piece!

We went to the Depot and rode the North Shore Scenic Railroad (dogs allowed), then the kids explored the museum while Gerry rolled along with his walker and I walked Atticus.

Duluth reminds me of other Great Lakes cities I've visited in Ohio, New York and Michigan; it seems less  *Minnesotan* to me. Folks seem to be rushing, maybe because it's *colder* here? I've seen a lot more impatient drivers. *I may be traumatized by my cab ride.*

After, the kids were worn out at the Depot we checked into our rental and were immediately hit with house envy. This is one *huge* house! Lots of room, two bathrooms on the second floor and a powder room on the ground floor. It's a house that needs a few more kids, and we feel oddly alone *[sigh]*. But we'll get by in the luxury surroundings, somehow.

The end of the yard a cliff overlooks Lake Superior, but there's a rustic staircase down to the pebble shore which I'm sure Atticus and the kids will explore today.

JUNE TWENTY-SIXTH
REMEMBER THE FIGHTS,
REMEMBER THE FUN...
DULUTH, MN

One of the suckiest *(is that a word?)* things about this whole *mishigas* are the frayed nerves. Mine, Gerry's, the kids, the dog's – everyone's.

We try not to let stuff get to us, but it does. Gerry's pissed off because – well, wouldn't *you* be? Suddenly the guy who was the tallest in his family has shrunk several inches. And that's the easy part.

I'm pissed because – well – because I'm tired and at the end of my rope. Luckily, I know how to tie a big, fat knot in that rope. I can even knit a little hammock chair to sit in, so the end of my rope is a relatively comfortable place to be. I'm settled in for a long swing.

Stress sucks. It would be so nice to live in a made-for-- TV Hallmark movie where everyone deals with tragedy with tears and hugs.

I'm taking a little mini-vacation from our vacation with the guy I love more than anything, who can't seem to see anything good in what I'm doing these days. *A little positive reinforcement, fella, would go a long way.*

I can't blame him. All he can clearly see is the pain and the black fogginess that is our immediate future. I figure just about everyone has days they're not too proud of. Today is one for both of us.

I got hailed on today. There was a bad storm as we were driving along Lake Superior. I'm sure that's where some of the stress came from, it was pretty scary.

And a teaching engagement that I'd planned on briefly reneged. (They were fearful that I would have to back out). But after some emails back and forth we're back on. Yay.

It's not the first time. I've lost other engagements recently when a shop or guild thoughtfully disengaged me, assuming my *place* was with Gerry.

One shop that cancelled wrote that they're *praying* for us. *I didn't have the nerve to write back and ask that they include a prayer for our mortgage, too.*

June Twenty-Eighth

Incredibly

Beautiful!

Duluth, MN

Yesterday was our driving-up-the-coast day, and we picked a good one for it! No more hailstorms, hardly even a dark cloud. We romped and splashed and climbed on rocks, Atticus joined us and loved every minute of it. *(Although he was a little worried when his "pups" crossed over a waterfall to a rock and he couldn't follow).*

97

Gooseberry Falls is as lovely as everyone said it would be, and the paved path made it a handicapped-friendly adventure. Best part of the day: when Gerry agreed that next year, when he's feeling better, he'll be able to climb across the falls, too! Actually, this is the best part of the vacation so far – the hopeful feeling that we all seemed to gain just by being in such beautiful surroundings.

Our fracas the other night was necessary, it helped clear the air and we discussed things that needed to be discussed. We felt like our old selves as we drove around yesterday. (Although at one point, my mind was so crammed with stuff that after paying for my gas I drove off without taking the nozzle out of the tank...) That was my *I Love Lucy* moment for the day. It didn't seem that any damage was done, but I guess we'll hear from the BP guy if there was.

We're blown away with the beauty around the Duluth area. The scenery is absolutely breathtaking, like walking through a postcard, and the weather yesterday was perfect! We met very friendly folks along the way and a few nice doggies, too.

Then we continued up to Split Rock lighthouse. I carried the walker up a flight of stairs and Gerry pulled himself up to enjoy the view. Continuing on we had a terrific lunch, chicken for the kids, a burger for Gerry and walleye for me. I even got my non-fish-eating kids to try it and admit they sort of liked it!

Those who know me know of my fear of flying, stinging insects. I'm finally okay around bees *(it's taken me 40-mumble years to get to this point),* but wasps and hornets paralyze me with fear. So imagine my horror when I looked out onto the back porch yesterday and saw not one, but *two* hornets nests.

"Oh," I thought, *"surely they're not active..."*

Then a hornet flew out of one and onto the other.

So I contacted the house owner about it, and when we returned from our trek north the hives had been smashed from the rafters (using my walking stick from the day before) and our "friends" are now looking for a new summer home.

It's a shame to make them give up their lakeside retreat, but we're paying more rent than they are.

JUNE THIRTIETH
RULE OF FIVES
DULUTH, MN

Duluth has a way of growing on you.

At first I thought the bridge was ungodly ugly, and tried to think of various ways a concerned municipality could circumvent this metal monstrosity.

But a funny thing happened as we drove and walked around Duluth – I started to *like* the bridge. I liked how often it goes up and down, I liked the little building next to it and the lighthouses at the end of the canal piers. And I began to actually appreciate the skeleton of the structure itself. So my *"Rule of Fives"* worked this time.

RULE OF FIVES

I've long thought that if we allow ourselves five of anything – five days in a new place, five dates with a new guy, five repeats of a new stitch pattern – that that should be long enough to determine our true feelings about it.

In general, we're too quick to make judgments. (I thought long and hard before writing that last sentence, don't judge it too quickly.) Anything that can make us pause, reflect and rethink is all for the good.

Most decisions don't need to be made as quickly as we've come to think they do. We've had decades of *split second decision making* being touted as a positive character trait, but I think that most important decisions slowly evolve from a set of facts. That is, if we give them *time*.

That's how my most successful designs have transpired. I have a spark of an idea, I don't lock myself into *one* direction with the idea, but work it out in a few different scenarios until something just feels right. When I do make a snap judgment, there is a good chance that I will

have to go back and revise it (I do *a lot* of revision).

With the luxury of working through something slowly, designing actually goes more quickly in the long run. That's irony.

Five months into the illness, Gerry's cancer is turning out to be the same way. The initial knee jerk reaction is that it sucks, it's awful and there's NO good that can come from it.

Well the first two things *are* certainly true. It DOES suck, it IS awful, and my mind alternatively reels and shuts down when I consider the various possible outcomes.

But after living with this for five months – as of July it will be five months since we became aware that something more serious than a *"bad back"* was probably at the heart of Gerry's constant pain – I'm seeing a different side to this whole journey.

A friend sent this quote to me, and it speaks volumes to my current state of mind:

> *"When it is dark enough, you can see the stars."*
> — Ralph Waldo Emerson

The stars we've been seeing lately are the hundreds of folks who are writing with good wishes and help. I write back to each one telling them that their good wishes and thoughts are the best gift we could receive.

July

St. Paul, MN

The sky here in Minnesota is absolutely beautiful. Watching the clouds is better than watching a movie. The weather changes, the clouds are so alive and active. It looks like rain over the next few days, we could use it, and I'm anxious to see the show.

Returning from vacation and getting back into our routine has been a grounding for my mind. I'm feeling like a St. Pauler *(St. Pauli?)*. Walking down Fairmount after dropping the kids off at camp, waving to folks I see just about every day, stopping to pet another dog (while trying to keep Atticus from becoming too – *ahem* – friendly).

All of these things make me feel as if I'm in the right place at the right time. I think the kids and Gerry feel this way, too. They say they do, but when there's such an upheaval in our lives it's hard to know for certain how we feel about anything.

I stopped by the Bravo Bakery today and sitting outside was a mom with her two children. She looked *so* much like my friend Ami from New Jersey that I had a little wave of homesickness.

We chatted briefly. They just moved here, and I found myself telling her about some of the great things on Grand Avenue, and what a wonderful place this is. I felt like a native. Well, maybe not entirely like a native, but pretty *durned* close.

The Long Run

He looks like Gerry, he sounds like him and has the same sense of humor, but I have the nagging feeling that it's not really my husband sitting in the kitchen or lying next to me in bed.

I want to shake him, *"Who are you, and what have you done with my husband?"* But that would be useless. I might as well look into a mirror and ask, *"Who am I, and where did Annie go?"*

Gerry has so much pain, it runs through his body and announces itself with every movement. He's taking Oxycontin, but – being a 12-hour medicine – it tends to get him in trouble. He'll take it and in an hour or so feel well enough to make plans to do this, or go there. Then a few hours later the medication begins to wear away and I can see on his face and in his posture how much pain he's trying to hide.

But he *wants* to do so much, and it's hard to convince him that he can't right now. I don't think it's a male/emasculating thing. It's the feeling that one does *not* want to be considered useless.

Unfortunately, it means more work for me – or, rather, more stress. It feels like when the kids were just old enough to get into trouble if left alone.

I worry that Gerry will want to go for a drive, go shopping, mow the lawn, and it will put him in a dangerous situation. Or perhaps I'll have to come and finish a job he's started and can't finish. I've seen how doing what used to be the most elementary of physical tasks wears him down and makes his pain worse.

It's a vicious circle. When I can get him to sit and rest, he feels well enough to do stuff. But then he wears out so quickly, his tremendous pain increases, and I have to become involved. The mental wear and tear is hardest to handle; jumping the emotional hurdles, making him feel needed, strong and necessary.

I try to help him understand that the way he can be *most* helpful is to rest his body so I can get more work done. And that sounds like such a slap in the face.

I feel like a prison warden *(haircut notwithstanding).*

Convincing him that he is *far* from useless is a hard dance. I can tell him to do this, or don't do that, and it just sounds like so much nagging. Gerry has to be the one to give himself permission to slow down a bit, and he has yet to be that kind to himself.

This is when I wish he had some male friends around who could come over and hang out, occupy his mind and shoot the shit so he's not talking to the radio.

How we'd *all* like some more time around here.

July Sixth

Clarify (& Justify?)

St. Paul, MN

Cancer isn't fun. It's rotten, mean and sneaky.

But in one of those insane ironies it's also been an odd kind of blessing. It's forced us to see how lucky we are: Things are not dire for us, we are among the luckiest people in the world. We have a good home, indoor plumbing, hot water, all the food we could want and things to amuse us (like knitting!).

105

We also have each other, and the fact that Gerry and I even found each other is a minor miracle. But we did, and we're lucky.

When my brother died a few years ago at age 44, I told my sister-in-law that it was tragic, but not a tragedy. The tragedy would have been if he hadn't met her, and they hadn't had 14 good years together.

We don't know how this will end, but we're hopeful that by preparing for the worst and hoping for the best, we will find the best in both of us. If we didn't have a good attitude and a good sense of humor (which, thank heaven, we both have), we'd be totally lost now.

Our jokes and laughter are like the white stones we can follow through this dark and scary forest of cancer back to some kind of normality.

It's good to note that Gerry is light years better than he was in March when we had no idea what he had. For years Gerry has suffered with ulcerative colitis, which tends to rear its ugly head sporadically. At the onset of the cancer Gerry was in the middle of a several-months-long bout of UC, and he was so exhausted, tired and in so much pain that we both felt rather hopeless. This was before we knew he had cancer. We just knew something was *seriously* wrong.

One of the drug therapies that's been helpful for Multiple Myeloma is a combination of Deximethezone and Thalidomide. This cocktail has not only been helpful with MM, it's also been working wonders with his ulcerative colitis.

A colonoscopy in April showed how well it's been working, and he's better in that regard than he's been in a *long* time! Not being able to get up and down stairs quickly, combined with ulcerative colitis, is a very hard thing to live with and creates episodes that are painfully embarrassing as well as just plain painful.

Right now Gerry's trying to wrap his mind around the fact that he's lost much of his bone density and these changes are irreversible. He was never a tall man, but he's 3" shorter than he was in February. I'm trying to keep him focused on the future, but he has to come to terms with what he's lost before we can move ahead.

July Seventh

Time Out & Time In

St. Paul, MN

I'm running away today.

I packed my two little bags and I got as far as the local Caribou Coffee *(which was actually my final destination)*. I've settled in, a cup of tea, a scone and later a frosty chocolate drink.

Three hours later I'm still here, getting more work done in the air-conditioning than I could have achieved in hours in our steamy, humid home. Thank heaven the folks are nice about me hanging around. I lend local color (well, my current project *is* intarsia).

It's hot here. It's hot *everywhere*. It's July 7th, day of the Live Earth Concert, and anyone who says the climate hasn't altered in the past century is a fool or a liar.

There, I've said it. Don't be shocked, I also believe in evolution. And gravity (both are theories). I continue to be amazed that out of the nine men running for the Republican nomination, three say they don't believe in it. (Evolution, not gravity – although I have my doubts.)

But I digress. I'm obviously enjoying the air-conditioning waaaay too much. Perhaps it's the eccentric

107

guy with red suspenders, a fixture at this Caribou Coffee, who hums to himself and plays with a rubber ducky while he sits at the table next to me. I wonder if the ducky believes in evolution?

He was annoying to me when he first walked in, but I've become used to him. Now he's bouncing a rubber ball and it's weirdly soothing. A very chic couple came in and scowled at him. I found myself feeling defensive for him. *(I didn't say anything, but I was fully prepared to scowl back at them if they looked over at me in solidarity.)*

So while I've been sitting here I've completed the *VK* intarsia shawl, except for crochet chain stitch "fringe" around the edge of the piece, and I'm ready to go home and give it a good steam block. Which seems absolutely redundant given the temperature in our house. The walk back home will probably block the darned thing.

After Monday we go back to the 80s during the day, 50/60s at night, yay!

It's *much* nicer to work on a wool shawl with lots of embroidery in a cool place – and now it's pretty much done and I'm pretty much happy.

I'll be teaching in Michigan and Ontario in early August and returning to St. Paul the day before we go down to Rochester. It will be air-conditioned at the Mayo.

It's so hard to try to project the whole future-with-Gerry thing. In the immediate future, I have to decide if I can fulfill my engagements or cancel them. I still have to earn a living, and the teaching keeps me connected and sane in a way other parts of my life don't.

Most of the shops where I'm scheduled to teach have gone out of their way to write and say, "We know things are up in the air now – we're willing to wait to hear how they turn out, and we hope for the best!"

I am SO grateful to these shops. I know how hard the waiting and not knowing is for me – I can't expect a yarn shop owner to bear the same burden of not knowing.

And here's a new lesson. I'd never thought of it before, but now I know exactly what someone in my position needs to hear:

"We'll wait for you, we're here for you, don't feel pressured to give us guarantees that you can't make."

The fact that so many yarn shop owners instinctively know to write and say this is a tremendous gift. The kindness of yarn shops is amazing.

Go visit your local yarn shop – it's probably air-conditioned!

July Tenth
Perfect Fit
St. Paul, MN

For a knitter, good fit is prime. There's that great moment when a finished sweater is tried on, the sleeves are long enough, the waist fits, the neckline sits at the right place; life is good!

I feel like I'm wearing that sweater today.

Today was a wonderful day. We dropped the kids off at camp so that we could drive down to Rochester and check out some of the housing alternatives. We looked at several places, but hands down the best fit for our circumstance was Staybridge Suites. And, most important, we can have Atticus with us.

We still haven't locked into one contractor for the great  kitchen divide, and against all good advice we may be moving away from Mr. Proven Contractor to Mr. Younger Flexible Contractor. Tomorrow Mr. YFC is coming by with his plumber so we can get a final quote.

In June, Max accidentally broke a large yellow-ware bowl that I loved. I saved all of the pieces because I just couldn't bear to part with it. We have an old 1920s hutch we acquired when we were first married in Brooklyn. It's not in great shape – to say it's shabby chic would be kind. It is built in two parts with a two-drawer bottom and a glass-door china cabinet top.

The bottom is counter height, so I'm thinking I'd like to create a lip around the edge with some type of molding. We'll cut a hole in the top of the hutch to accommodate the sink, then I'll take the pieces from the beloved yellow-ware bowl, break them into even

smaller pieces, and use them
to create a mosaic pattern around the hole.

Once that's finished and grouted, I'll cover all of it with
polyurethane to make the top flat and even. The
molding lip will hold the bar-pour in place. I may even
toss in some other stuff, other dish shards, pennies,
shells, stitch markers... Will it work? Who knows!

If it does we end up with a groovy, expressive sink for
peanuts. If not, we haven't lost that much.

Driving back home from Rochester the landscape was
breathtaking. I've never seen corn look as beautiful as it
did along Highway 52. Lush and tall and 50 shades of
green. The sky was a deep, rich Dutch blue. The light on
the fields, the wind moving the grasses and stalks, it
almost made me cry.

We got home just in time to sign for a delivery, check
my email (*Vogue* is very happy with the shawl – yay!),
and I changed my clothes and strolled over to the
Yarnery to meet some new friends for knitting at Cafe
Latte. I have missed connecting with a group of knitters
as a knitter, not teacher, just Annie.

One of the women's husband had a stem cell transplant
five years ago and is doing great after being "*given*" three
years. Love to hear that.

As I walked home at 9:30 p.m., the sky still light with
northern evening brightness, I felt so at home, so happy.
Back at the house Gerry was snoring in his recliner, the
kids were getting ready for bed, the cat and dog asleep
in the living room snuggled next to each other. *(It's just
chilly enough for some good pet snuggling.)*

What a nice fit.

THINGS THAT GROW

The sky is blue, the sun is shining, and – the best part – the temperature is in the upper 70s. I can take just about anything but heat. Right now I'm in heaven.

Walking the kids to camp every day we pass so many amazing gardens. Beautiful yards, plants, flowers, a fence made entirely of cultivated apple trees. Folks here *love* their greens!

Hannah's taller, Max's shoulders are filling out, our kids are growing. You don't notice it for a while, then one day it just dawns on you how tall your kids really are. Hannah's almost taller than Gerry right now.

I had put off contacting yarn shops where I'm teaching this Fall. I'm finally writing to each venue offering to gracefully let them off the hook if the idea of waiting for me to possibly cancel is just too nerve-wracking.

A yarn shop is a narrow-margin business. Not many yarn shops owners I know are getting rich; most are happy to keep body and soul together and pay the rent. I understand that between the extra planning and advertising and any other costs that may come up when engaging an outside teacher, it may be too much to expect a shop to keep dates open for me if I can't guarantee that I'll be there to teach.

I think I've put this off because the *only* reason I'd be canceling is if things don't go well with the Blood and Marrow Transplant. I don't want to think about that.

But the head can't stay under the pillow forever, and it's necessary to deal with this possibility in terms of how it will affect the shops that have hired me sooner rather than later. The sad truth is, cancer comes at inconvenient times – but bills still have to be paid!

I am *definitely* planning on being in France for the French Girl Knits retreat. The tickets have been purchased, I'm arranging child care coverage for those weeks, and dang it – I just *want* to go. Gerry will be finishing up his time in Rochester, his mom is flying in and she'll be taking care of him during my absence. His sister will fly in and stay with the kids in St. Paul.

The Mayo Clinic does Bone Marrow Transplants as an out-patient procedure, but Gerry MUST stay in a hotel in the immediate area. That's why we'll have to pay for six to eight weeks of hotel coverage.

Having said that, I can't deny that as the worry of running through our savings to cover accommodation expenses while Gerry's at the Mayo Clinic diminishes, I find myself much more able to focus on what truly is important in life.

This week the insurance company for Gerry's former employer has finally agreed to pay short-term disability. They had been insisting that since that first doctor misdiagnosed the condition and wrote a note stating that Gerry would be out of work for only four days, this was the only diagnosis they *had* to accept. *Insanity.*

But apparently the letters from Gerry's oncologist and our primary care physician have finally convinced them to relent. So we'll be the proud recipients of $170 per week, the New York State minimum, *among the lowest in the country we're told.*

Interestingly, this involved a form which Gerry's general practitioner was required fill out and which had to be returned within a certain number of days or we'd lose our eligibility. Gerry had a funny feeling about it so we stopped over to the doctor's office to see if the form had arrived. We discovered that it *had*, but with *none* of Gerry's information included with it.

The doctor's office had no idea for whom the form was to be filled out. It's hard for me to believe, given the time sensitive nature of this form, that leaving Gerry's info off was entirely accidental.

Cynicism grows like a tumor, too!

JULY SIXTEENTH
THE RUNNING OF THE POODLES
WOODBURY, MN

We had such a wonderful visit with friends this weekend – and it occurred to Gerry and me that we hadn't *been* to anyone's house for a cookout type thing since we left South Orange!

It's hard for Gerry to get around, hard to feel 100% comfortable anyplace but our house. But in preparation for the Blood and Marrow Transplant he's coming off of his meds one at a time, and I think he's becoming a little more serious about the pain meds. He was feeling good enough to go out to a friend's house in Woodbridge for some grilled burgers, poodle running and kid playing!

Mostly it was just nice to see Gerry able to get out and be part of the WORLD. I know how isolated he feels, so this was really great for him. After a few hours he was so exhausted that the pain was creeping into his bones, and we had to hit the road.

We just dropped Hannah and Max off at Phalen Lakeside for canoeing and kayaking day camp. We love the St. Paul recreation centers. Gerry insists that he wants to drive over and pick up the kids if I'm in the middle of something at 3:00 p.m. when camp is out. But I worry about his driving with the pain meds.

And – truth be told – *he does, too.*

July Seventeenth
Finding Things
St. Paul, MN

I'm starting to clean out the kitchen, get appliances and unused dishes squared away a little at a time. The same way I packed the house oh, about six months ago. Feels like yesterday. *Feels like 100 years ago.*

Max found his sweet spot and he's finally figured out how to connect with the ball. Although he's not hitting homers, he's making *hits*! I keep telling him I'd be proud of him no matter how he did, but it's a thrill to see his happy face running to base. All the way home from the ballpark on Monday he told me about his strategy to hit against the pitchers. Who knew my son knew from strike zones?

Gerry rode with me to pick up the kids from Lake Phalen today, they're *loving* the canoeing and kayaking!

As we drove home we found a few of our friends out on their front lawn, so a brief stop and a kid exchange ensued and we had an impromptu playdate. This feels so good I can hardly express it.

While the kids played, I rearranged the front porch. It was hot, I was pushing and pulling and lifting and carrying – so hot. After all that work I hobbled into the kitchen to get a Diet Coke, aching, in pain, exhausted.

And it dawned on me; *this is how Gerry feels 95% of the time.*

JULY EIGHTEENTH

LOST SLOTS

ST. PAUL, MN

Worry is weird – obviously we're not starving, and we have enough equity in our home to take out a loan to add a bathroom for Gerry. *Gotta love the equity.*

BUT, we've worked for 20 years to *get* that equity – and we realize that the way things are going we may be eating in to that equity in a very large way in the next few years.

As my mother would say, *"That's why we earn it..."* But is it? Did we earn it to drop so much on costs involved in a serious illness? So that a healthcare CEO can earn 419 times more than the woman who cleans the toilets in his office? It adds insult to injury to realize the way our system is set up, we're simply helping the insurance company execs become as rich as humanly possible. *Or would that be as rich as inhumanely possible.*

Conspiracy Alert: I think it's all part of a larger plan to destroy the middle class and create a new lower-lower middle class of folks so broke and poor due to health care costs *(biggest reason for personal bankruptcy!)* that they're willing to take *any* job that includes healthcare. Then we can finally compete with China to make those

2¢ American Flags the rich folks' kids will put on their bikes for the July 4th parade.

We are the face of the race to last place.

Actually, I'm not sure if I am such a conspiracy theorist – or maybe I am *(hmmm, what's your theory on that)*. But I do think there are powerful entities working to retain the status quo, and the status quo is – quite literally – killing us.

Just keep repeating to yourself, *"We're the wealthiest nation in the world, we're better than this."* Because we are.

Then tell yourself, *"I'm the most powerful person in this country, I have a vote."* Because you **do**.

When I was so sick four years ago we ran up a ton of medical and non-medical expenses. (We didn't have insurance, and although my doctor treated me *gratis*, she couldn't get my drugs or X-rays, etc. for free.) But we got through by taking out loans and living *very* frugally.

When we sold our house in New Jersey this past year we made enough on it to pay off the loans we'd taken out at that time. Nothing like a fresh start, huh? It feels like a brutal poetic *in*justice to have this cancer hit us just when we felt a bit free and clear.

Lesson: *Perhaps we're not meant to be free and clear.*

Better Lesson: *This wouldn't be an issue if we lived in almost any other industrialized nation.*

Bitter Lesson: *Perhaps no one is EVER really free and clear, and this is the impetus we need to keep us striving...?*

It's a theory.

George Bernard Shaw felt that a person's unhappiness was in direct proportion to how much they had above or below their needs. The very rich and the very poor are both unhappy – only those who have what they need (and not too much or too little) are truly happy. I tend to agree with that.

I've cut down on my teaching, writing and designing so much that it's really scary at times. And sometimes shops kindly help me out by cutting my teaching down for me – this evening I received a note that read:

> *[We] thought that to pressure you this Spring with your family issues was not a good idea. Therefore, we let your teaching assignment ride. We recently filled that time slot and that takes care of us for this calendar year.*

Hey – thanks for the heads up!

It was a surprise, to say the least. I guess it does make it easier when I don't have to make those hard decisions like *"should I teach this Fall? "* myself. That *is* a weight off my mind!

To be honest, if we're not approved for Social Security Disability, I have *no* idea what we'll do. *Oh, who cares, I have three full cartons of Diet Coke left, and I'm wild with a chemical high!*

But if SSD doesn't come through we'll apply again. And we'll get through. We'll borrow, we'll find help, I'll work my butt off, I'll write a best selling book about this and they'll make a movie. Renée Zellweger will play me *(she'd be able to gain the necessary weight)*. Bob Hoskins can play Gerry.

– *"You had me at 'I love beer!'"*

We'll become rich, Gerry will be 100% better, and the kids will have no cavities.

But then the tension and stress from all that extra money will make us fuss and feud, and eventually our newfound wealth will cause us to divorce.

So see how lucky we are now? And with our newly organized front porch, we're living the high life.

July Nineteenth
Fun Stuff
St. Paul, MN

So we've picked a contractor. It's Mr. Younger-But-Enthusiastic Contractor – tada! Gerry's been elected to tell Mr. Established Contractor we're not going with him. He has the whole pathos thing going, and we think he won't get yelled at. We're really losing a good bet by not taping this kitchen redo for a reality show on HGTV, *Remodeling with Cancer*!

Our current kitchen is appliance poor – part of why the price of the house was so low. We're not setting out to "flip" the house or anything, but that same nagging feeling that told me (Okay, *yelled* at me!) that we should move to the Twin Cities is telling me to be intelligent and thorough in any upgrades we do. *I hear and I obey.*

Earlier folks were asking, *"When are we going to see the FUN stuff – the colors for the kitchen, etc..."*

Well, you asked for it, here it is. I saw a photo of a house that was for sale and liked the feeling so much that we're trying to match it with our own kitchen. It seems good for the period (1918) and doable on a budget without sacrificing style. *Please don't tell me that I have no business enjoying this part of it, I can't help it.*

Doing something cheaply and badly won't be a help to anyone in the long run. As we said to our contractor – we'd like to be frugal – but not cheap.

Tonight was another ball game. Max gets a lot of good male attention, he's bonding with teammates, and he's finally figured out how to hit the ball. Every time at bat tonight he connected, getting a double three times and

making it home twice.

Hannah showed me that she can do something I have *never* been able to mistress – whistling through a blade of grass! And she's GOOD!

After the game Hannah, Max and I walked over to Grand Ol' Creamery and bought cones, then we walked home on this lovely and cool evening.

There's something about a couple of redheaded kids, one in a Dodgers baseball uniform, eating ice cream cones and whistling through grass that makes the whole world smile.

Well, it made the folks we passed on Grand Avenue smile.

JULY TWENTY-SECOND
Yo, YO!
ST. PAUL, MN

My breathing sucks today. My breathing is also bad because last night my next door neighbors decided to set off all of their leftover fireworks, the wind was blowing toward us, our fans were on and the house was saturated with that gun-powdery smell in seconds. It lasted for hours. *Thanks guys.*

My neighbor is a funny kid. I don't know him at all, but I hear him on the phone, swearing a lot, talking like a *gangsta*, yelling at his girlfriend (at least, I'm assuming that's who *"Bee-yotch"* is).

The first time I heard him say, *"Yo, yo, wassup mah n---"* I thought he was saying, *"Yo, yo, wassup mah knittah!"*

Obviously my mind is always on fiber. *Well, it seemed appropriate for Minnesota... And bear in mind this neighbor is so white he makes ME look "café au lait!"*

Thank heaven I have a nebulizer, which I used to good effect this morning. Minnesota health care is a marvelous thing. Back in New Jersey I'd just wheeze all day, then get very scared and maybe end up in the emergency room later in the evening.

I probably could have obtained a nebulizer, but my pulmonary doctor never brought it up, and the whole insurance thing just seemed more – *daunting* – back there. *Running the gauntlet of sometimes-not-so-nice medical staff was daunting, too.*

Here, my doctor asked me if I'd like to have a nebulizer, and her office did up the paperwork and I picked it up a few days later. I've only used it twice since then, but those were bad days and they saved me (and our insurance company) an expensive, scary and time-consuming trip to the ER.

Preventative health investment, what a concept.

Me Time

No matter how much I walk, or how careful I try to be with the eating, I feel that my body shape is sort of frozen right now.

It seems that there are times when weight just falls off, and there are times when it won't come off with a hammer and chisel. This current period of heat and stress is one of the latter – and it will pass – but it's rough now.

I'm not too concerned with it. Aside from the breathing, I feel very healthy in my current routine. I'm walking a lot, getting a lot done, doing a nice amount of physical work and I feel good. But I don't feel *thin*. Every year in August I feel so logy, then in the Fall I slim down without really trying very hard, so I know this will pass. But it bothers me. *And it bothers me that it bothers me.*

I think it's due to many factors – the societal pressure to be thin, my own desire to wear pretty clothes, wanting folks to think well of me when they first meet me. And, perhaps most troubling, the fact that my husband has *"shrunk"* – he's a good 5" shorter than he was a few months ago, 8" shorter than me.

I feel so very exposed when we're together. I find myself explaining to folks I've just met why I'm so much taller than Gerry. Not good for either of our egos. I know that this makes him feel handicapped – lesser in some way – and I need to stop it. It's ridiculous to allow my vanity to cause Gerry pain.

But it's hard to be a walking sight gag. I've often joked that in our society the worst thing a woman can do is take up too *much* space; the worst thing a man can do is take up too *little*.

I don't mean that seriously, of course – and things have changed a lot (for the better) since I was a teenager. But there's that feeling that it's just not quite *feminine* to be too big. Or, to follow the panty hose corollary, the taller a woman is, the less she is allowed to weigh.

I break that rule. I'm simultaneously happy, proud, ashamed and irritated by my looks. I think we *all* are. I'm upset that a bias against fat is still strong, and accepted by folks who would never engage in sexist or racist comments. The last acceptable bias.

But on the other hand, I feel that there's a growing movement of pride in our bodies, no matter what their shape and size. And I love those Dove soap ads with all the different shaped women.

In the shower, soon after I delivered Max, I remember thinking, *"How can I hate a body that has given me two such wonderful babies?"*

And speaking of vanity, I'm almost finished with the sink top for the bathroom. It's grouted and the edging is in place.

I've run a bead of silicone around the inside of the mosaic area to act as a dam when I pour the polyurethane on tomorrow, then I'll let it sit for a few days.

It's truly been a labor of love, it has made me so happy to make this for the bathroom. I hope it turns out that we really CAN use the vanity top!

Hannah leaves on Sunday morning for Girl Scout camp. We had signed the kids up for these various camps (canoe camp, invention camp, Girl Scout camp) in March, before Gerry's diagnosis. I felt it was necessary to pack the kid's first summer in Minnesota.

And as things turned out, giving them such a rich and full summer has been quite a blessing. It's kept all of our minds off of the seriousness of our situation. If there were ever a summer when it's important that the kids and Gerry make excellent memories, this is it! We'll take the joy wherever we can get it.

It means the world to Gerry to see both kids having such a great summer – it makes us so happy to see them adjusting well to St. Paul, making friends and finding cool stuff to do. We don't dwell a lot on Gerry's sickness. But it trails us, breaking into conversations like an excited child.

When it became clear how serious Gerry's illness was, and what this would mean for us financially, I contacted the different camps to see about getting a refund. With only one exception, they each offered us partial scholarships so the kids could stay in their various programs. I was so grateful – we are all so grateful.

I'd never imagined there was as much kindness as we've been shown since Gerry's diagnosis, and it's difficult to know exactly how to feel. Grateful doesn't seem big enough.

For the rest of our lives we'll never pass a barn-raising without stopping to help.

JULY TWENTY-NINTH
LONDON CALLING
ST. PAUL

London's cousin, Kingston

Today a new friend, London, came over to help us empty the kitchen for the contractors. But I'd moved a lot of stuff this morning into the dining room so when London arrived, ready to work, I was tired and ready to sit and chat and knit. She agreed. *No work for YOU!*

Gerry came downstairs and joined us, and for the first time we talked in detail about his procedure. Oddly, we don't often speak about it, so chatting with London was good for everyone. The Mayo had sent a DVD outlining the blood and marrow transplant process in graphic detail. It's very informative, but both of us wish that there were more real interviews with actual patients and caregivers.

I can hardly believe that in a week we'll be going down to Mayo, and I'm scared for Gerry. Not scared in a long-term sense as much as just wanting any discomfort or pain to be as minimal as possible. It feels as though we're about to enter a long, long, dark tunnel. I have to let Gerry go first because it's his journey – he can intuit the way better than I.

All I can do is follow close behind and hold the flashlight straight.

JULY THIRTY-FIRST
60 MORE DAYS OF WAITING
ST. PAUL, MN

Every day is a new lesson – our lesson today:

What's a Disability Quality Branch?

The DQB, or disability quality branch, is the Social Security Administration's version of quality control when it comes to the handling of Social Security Disability and SSI-disability claims.

But why should WE care? [chord of ominous music]

> *A random number of disability claims (for which decisions have already been rendered) are selected each month for "review" at each region's DQB. Cases pulled by DQB for review can remain there for an inordinate number of weeks or even months. The obvious effect of this is that some cases are significantly delayed by DQB (decision letters cannot be mailed until DQB has finished reviewing a case).*

> *Information courtesy www.disabilitysecrets.com*

You know what's coming, right? We were supposed to have the decision on Gerry's Disability claim by the end of July. Today is the end of July, so when we didn't hear anything from SSI Gerry called and we discovered his application has been chosen at random to make sure that all the i's are dotted and the t's are crossed.

How odd that they didn't arrive in a van at our front steps with a bunch of balloons and a TV crew to announce that to us...

We were told to expect at least a 60-day wait before we hear anything, so we're looking at October before we get the word. Now THAT'S how we put someone's mind at rest when they're about to undergo a serious medical procedure. We're not feeling killer worried – well, we're trying not to – because the Social Worker at the Mayo told us that a Bone Marrow Transplant is pretty much an automatic approval from SSI.

Note: SSI is not impressed by the phrase, "But the social worker at the Mayo said we'd be approved!" Especially not when you say it in a really whiny voice. Live and learn.

So until we hear positive news, we'll just keep on keeping on. In that vein, we're getting a HELOC (Home Equity Line of Credit) with Gerry's bank. It's a good rate with no fees, and we can use it as we need it for the bathroom/kitchen redo. We'd always planned on it, now it makes even more sense. We need to continue to think of this as an investment in Gerry's recovery.

Max played on the Dodgers this summer (we kept pretending they were the Brooklyn Dodgers) and, lo and behold, the Dodgers won the Linwood Recreation Center Championship!

We had a TOTAL Red Barber moment up in the cheap seats at the recreation center last evening. It was so exciting to see how Max improved over this Summer, how he went from striking out pretty consistently to finding the spot on the bat that needed to be hit.

Last evening he made a great play from second base and Gerry said he had more RBIs than anyone else. I'm not quite sure what that means, but Max was happy! We took him to Snuffy's for dinner – he told the waitress, *"If it wasn't for me, my team would have had to finish the 9th inning!"* Who knew?

His coach is an amazing guy, the nicest, sweetest, most confidence-building coach a kid could ask for, and it's been a pure gift that Max got him this summer. We've been so lucky. And next year Max can be on the same team, with the same great group of kids.

Hannah's at camp and we all miss her so much! Max is *not* as enchanted with being an only child as he thought he'd be. He's going to be very happy when she gets back.

I leave tomorrow to teach in Michigan and Canada. When I get home on Sunday night I'll have about 12 hours before we leave for Rochester. There is still so much to do. But we're in good shape with the packing – I'm just worried about getting the kids all ready to go off on their Jersey adventure on Wednesday. This is all happening so fast.

The vanity top is pretty much finished and the contractor is psyched about it, too! *So our groovy, artsy vanity cost us a grand total of $40.*

AUGUST

AUGUST FIRST
CRAZY WORRIED
SARNIA, ONTARIO, CANADA

Today was messed up; bumped from flight, gate change, killer traffic from Detroit to Canada and I was late for my lecture.

Where the hell is Gerry?

When I arrived at my hotel and turned on the TV and saw the news of the bridge collapse on 35W I immediately phoned Gerry, but I can't get hold of him. My cell phone battery is dying and I don't have a charger.

Where the hell is Gerry?

I keep telling myself, *"There's NO good reason why he'd be over by 35W..."* Except his brother is in town and they might have been doing some sight seeing. Max was with them today. I know they wanted to go see a ball game (the stadium is by the bridge).

I left the hotel number on our home answering machine, forcing myself to speak slowly and repeat the number twice. Obviously I cannot sleep until I hear from him. I'm supposed to teach at 9:00 a.m. tomorrow.

12:45 a.m. Update

He's home. They went to see a movie, they got home and got my message and called the hotel. My own cell is totally powerless now, but at least I know he's okay!

I am not a worrier, not usually. However, my deepest childhood fear is falling off of a bridge in a car and getting trapped in a river. Until just a few years ago I had never owned a car with electric windows *(they stop*

130

working in water). So my mind was filled with horrible images, and now I'm going to try to get five hours sleep so I can teach tomorrow.

I think so much of my pent up worry found its way into my active brain this evening.

AUGUST SECOND
SAFE & WELL
SARNIA, ONTARIO, CANADA

The Twin Cities are like a small town. Obviously they're the biggest cities in Minnesota and have all of the benefits of living in a city, but they feel more homey to me.

It's a very connected area, and I can only imagine the pain that everyone feels right now back home. This is how I know that the TC is finally becoming our home – I feel terrible to be away now. I wish I were there and could do something.

Listening to the TV last night, hearing the reporters conjecture on the folks who were trapped in cars – *"The myth of the air bubble isn't true..."* just turned me inside out. When I heard that Gerry was okay, I was so grateful. And then I laid awake all night thinking, *"There are at least 20 other families that are sleepless, worried, imagining the worst..."*

It is almost laughably cliché, but when Gerry dropped me off at the airport I didn't like the way he pulled up to the curb. I thought I was running late, I was stressed, and I snapped at him, *"Oh, just pull up for god's sake!"*

My last comments to him before I left were annoyed, and my goodbye kiss to him was grudging. I almost forgot to kiss poor Maxie, and it wasn't the loving mommy kiss I would have liked it to be. I'm so glad that's not the last physical connection we'll have.

AUGUST THIRD
SPINNING OUT
LANSING, MI

I miss home. I've only been gone a few days, and I miss it. I'm back in Michigan, about as homey as I can get in these 50 states since I was raised in Toledo, just south of the Michigan border, and lived briefly in Temperance, MI *(the perfect place for a Methodist)*.

But it's not home. Home is where Gerry and the kids are. Today Hannah gets back from Girl Scout camp, then they're all going to a Twins game.

Max's camp was supposed to go to the game yesterday, but it's been postponed for obvious reasons. And, also for obvious reasons, I can't get those missing folks out of my mind. Or their families. *I wish I were home.*

Nothing since 9/11 has felt so *much* like 9/11 to me, most likely because we live in the Twin Cities and I'm chomping at the bit to get home. The whole bridge collapse thing – and being away from Gerry at the same time – has unbalanced me, set me off my spin for a bit.

So I have to re-adjust, take some time to center myself, and get back into my usual rotation. Maybe I should take up spinning...

AUGUST SIXTH
BEARING THREADS
LANSING, MI

When I teach more than three classes at a venue I fear folks will get tired of my stock jokes, stories, the little songs I sing and my general *schtick*.

If the students at Threadbear were tired of me, they were kind (and gentle) enough not to let me know. Heaven knows I told the same damned jokes over and over, but there always seemed to be at least ONE person who hadn't heard it, and that was enough to allow everyone enjoy it all over again.

So much laughter, though, is wearying. So much teaching is rough. I think an hour of hardcore instruction is equivalent to three hours of design work. Teaching four days in a row is utterly exhausting.

On Saturday during *movie night* at the shop, I retired to my host's home to rest a bit and watch the fireworks at the ball field across the river. The Lansing Lugnuts know how to put on a good show! I called Gerry on my newly charged cell phone.

Gerry and I don't talk about it much, the *"bad"* possibility, but the understanding is so complete between ourselves that we don't need to discuss it. As I was falling asleep in an odd bed, alone, far from home, the implications of this whole thing socked me so hard it knocked the wind out of me – I couldn't even sob.

When I'm tired I become emotional. I was in tears when I said goodbye to Rob – so much sympathy, so much love from the students.

I can't figure out why I deserve so much love, but I will gladly take it. And I hope that I'm able to give it back with my full, whole heart soon!

Gerry just admitted to me that he's excited about our stay in Rochester, the stem cell transplant, everything. He paused and I completed his thought:

> *A – I'm excited, too – in a weird way.*
> *G – I was about to say the same thing!*
> *A – We've been married too long.*
> *G – Not long enough.*

August Seventh
Ladies & Gentlemen, Live from the Mayo!
Rochester, MN

Some of the music they play around here is pretty amusing. As we walked into our first appointment this morning, we heard the Longine Symphonette version of *"What Are You Doing The Rest Of Your Life?"* I'm not sure if anyone else caught it in the waiting room, it was a pretty florid arrangement and you had to listen carefully to understand it. Someone burning the CDs around here has a pretty good sense of humor.

A pianist plays in the lobby of the Mayo building during lunch hours, the pedestrians hurrying from one building to another passing in front of her piano, looking as if they're doing a crazy waltz.

This is the Grand Central Station of health. As Gerry and I turned a corner – me with the "step-side step-hop" that I always seem to be doing these days to avoid tripping over his wheels – I almost ran into an older man who smiled at me and said, "With this music we could be dancing!"

He had a strong, kind face. I found myself hoping that he was here for himself, and not for a loved one. I think deep down it's easier to deal with our own illness rather than see someone we love become very sick.

Watching people's faces is interesting. Older folks, those in their 70s and above, are relatively unfazed. Some seem to enjoy the activity and the very kind interactions with the Mayo staff. This must be the point in life when all that much touted wisdom and experience kick in and you realize that if you're just along for the ride, you may as well enjoy it!

Folks in their 40s to their 70s are either accompanying a younger family member *(in which case they look a lot better than I'd look, but still, they've got that "must get through this" set to their jaws),* or – like Gerry – they may be patients themselves. The patients are obvious because their accompanying party consists of a worried looking spouse, furrow-browed siblings or oblivious children.

Younger folks, in their 20s and 30s, seem to be the most upset – definitely the most irritated. If their time is cut short, then f'heaven's sake get *out* of their way! This makes sense, they are much too young to be seriously ill, or to lose someone to a serious illness. We're all too young.

There are a few kids, mostly children and grandchildren of patients. While we were waiting for Gerry's echocardiogram there were some siblings running amok, apparently waiting for Grandma, and their dad was obviously a "hands off" type of parent. It was the only time today a waiting room seemed loud.

135

The Mayo staff member who addressed the dad was *so* gracious and kind, I wish I had her diplomatic skills! I haven't seen many worried-looking children, thank heaven, *plenty of time for that later.*

I miss the kids. When I got back from Michigan and saw how happy Hannah was – confident and, I swear, taller – I knew that sending her to Girl Scout camp this summer was the BEST thing we could have done. I feel like we've equipped her with extra abilities to deal with the time away from us, and to be a source of comfort and strength for Max. She makes an excellent, if bossy, older sister.

I just kept knitting all day, even when the lights were turned out so the tech could do Gerry's echo *(knitting in the dark).* The knitting calms me, and soothes folks around me, too. It's easy to allow the knitting to take us to a meditative state where we can hover at the edge of our consciousness, not fully invested in the moment, but ready to leap up the minute a nurses calls, *"Landy, Gerard Landy!"*

What the artwork, kind folks, music and magazines can't obliviate is the knowledge that every one who is here is either involved with someone who is very sick, or is very sick themselves. And not just any old sick, *Mayo Sick.*

Mayo Sick is having been to another facility, and – perhaps as a last resort – finding your way here for the excellent care. This is not where folks come who have a simple urinary tract infection. Folks who come here seem to have been through the *system* and are scarred in various ways. But there's a lot more hope than worry on the faces I've seen.

Gerry and I? We're just giddy. We're usually pretty giddy together, even after almost 14 years, unless we're in pissy moods. Today we're scared, and that makes us laugh like nervous adolescents.

Gerry's first test was a bone marrow biopsy, which had been – to date – his most painful experience up in St. Paul.

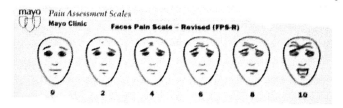

I delight in asking him, *"Painful, yes – but how does it compare to childbirth?"* You got nothing on me, Landy...

On the wall was an electronic billboard type of readout to help the staff keep track of what patient is in which room. Gerry said it was the Powerball numbers. I thought it was a new form of Bingo, "MAYO!" (It's only four letters, so it takes less time...)

What are YOU doing the rest of your life?

Gerry was out cold for the test and he's not supposed to make any legal decisions for the rest of the day. The procedure was quick, relatively pain-free, and he was up and coherent in 20 minutes, walking around as if he'd only had a nap. Amazing.

They do more blood and marrow transplants here than anywhere else. If you do something a lot you get good at all of the pre-procedure testing stuff. Anything that saves Gerry a bit of pain is fine with me!

So while Gerry's getting his teeth and jaw checked, I'm waiting patiently. It feels like forever. *And now they're playing, "Please Release Me." Dang.*

At one point today we rode the elevator with a mom and her teenage daughter who'd just finished her stem cell transplant experience and was heading home, bald but healthier than she *had* been and with a brighter outlook than the mom had expected. It was easy to see that the mom was just barely holding it together, the gratitude showing in every part of her face. As we parted, she said to me, *"He'll be okay, you'll see!"*

Which was a very nice thing for her to say. And an even better thing to hear. Just the connection with another Mom – another woman about my age – was a nice thing.

As forecast, knitting is EXCELLENT here at the Mayo, and I spied three other knitters as well as a woman at the information desk doing some interesting stuff with two needles and yarn. It makes me wonder if there's any regular knitting group at the Mayo.

I got Gerry to make three stitches today – it's progress – and maybe I can get him to finish a row tomorrow.

AUGUST TENTH

REFLECTIONS FROM THE MAYO CRUISE

ROCHESTER, MN

In the Mayo complex, whether by design or function, you feel as if you're on a journey. Waiting rooms look like train stations, the exam rooms have the feeling of a sleek 1940s sleeper car, and the atrium in the Mayo/ Gonda building is like the deck of a ship.

Today felt like the Mediterranean portion of our Mayo Cruise. There's an interesting-looking building on the hill across from our hotel. It appeared to be an Italian villa, *Tuscany in Minnesota*. We found out today it is the Convent of the Sisters of St. Francis. I wonder if there are tours.

I keep telling Gerry when I go to France in September everything will look like Minnesota to me. The first time I went to Belgium it looked so Ohio-esque. We view new things through the eyes we have, and now we have the unique opportunity to see only each other with the kids away and this time alone.

Our first appointment was pleasant and informative. We enjoyed meeting the nurse, she put us at ease and explained the full procedure quite clearly. Then we walked around, checking out the magnificent artwork. I *kvelled* at a Calder mobile, *Fish*.

I love Calder. There had been a Calder stabile in front of World Trade Center 7 when I worked there, and I had lunch near it as often as possible. When that building came down – empty – late in the day on 9/11, I wept for the Calder on top of tears for the souls in WTC 1 and 2.

One of the pieces in a Mayo elevator bank is an ancient Roman mosaic. I love it, the lines and strength make me happy. Seeing a detail from an early Roman piece makes it seem almost abstract, who knew how much I like abstract stuff?

Everyone here is so friendly, *so* clean cut with little black and white name plates. There are folks from all over the world here, so many examples of interesting and

beautiful cultural dress. I counted at least five different types of woman-wrapping garments yesterday.

There's an enormous sculpture of a man with a strategic fig leaf, but NO revealing sculptures of women. Actually, the few realistic representations of women I've seen are a bas relief showing nuns in traditional habit (some scrubbing floors) or sculptures of women as mothers and caregivers. *Interesting.*

A few Mennonites rode by on bikes as we walked home, more local flavor. I saw some women from a distance who appeared to be wearing 14th-century Dutch headdresses, I have to find them tomorrow and see exactly WHAT they have on!

After lunch we met with Dr. Costas again. He's here at the Mayo on a fellowship working in the Blood and Marrow transplant department and has become one of our favorite folks to chat with.

He's Brazilian, a very nice guy, and has an easygoing way of explaining complicated procedures so that we can understand them.

He has a slight accent, it seems ridiculous to even mention it since I can't imagine what kind of an accent I'd have if I tried to speak Portuguese.

He told Gerry that by the time we went home at the end of this entire procedure he'd only be taking a "cupful" of pills every day. (Having experienced this confusion before, I

immediately understood him to
mean "a couple," not *cupful*.)

So that's our goal. Brand spanking new stem cells and a
couple of pills a day in eight easy weeks.

AUGUST TWELFTH
HOLD THE MAYO
ROCHESTER, MN

At the Mayo there are signs near each elevator warning
that if you're sneezing or coughing, STAY AWAY. I
appreciate these signs – it will be a short time until
Gerry undergoes high-dose chemo and will be
susceptible to all kinds of viruses. I woke up with a
pretty strong sneezing, coughing, headachy cold this
morning and it's turned into a full flown chest cold. Lots
of coughing.

I'm going to take it easy for a day or so. Luckily, there's a
five day break while we wait for final approval from
Gerry's insurance company, so we'll be entirely away
from Mayo until Thursday, when Gerry begins getting
his growth hormone to create more stem cells. Gerry's
taking advantage of this by driving over to a grocery
store. I think he's relishing just being out alone,
something he's not done in weeks, and something
everyone needs. He's feeling better than he has in months,
so if he wants to get out and enjoy himself on his own,
all the better!

Last night on one of the Multiple Myeloma sites he
visits, a fellow announced that his wife just lost her MM
battle after three years. As we read his post it was a
somber moment for both of us. And, of course, we
asked each other, *"Was she taking the drugs I am?"*, *"Did she
have a blood and marrow transplant?"* But this is, after all is

141

said and done, a very individualistic disease. *Multiple Myeloma* has unintended meanings.

So if Gerry wants to run around buying staplers, laundry soap and small tripods *(he's creating a video diary of his experience)* then let him. Any small autonomy is good.

We drove over to Otawanna yesterday simply to get *out*. On the drive the weather was very odd, dark clouds in front of us with lightning flashing, but sunny behind where we had come from. The sun seemed to follow us, even when we headed into a brief shower we were in the sun.

We drove past a wind farm – Gerry'd never seen one before. In Duluth we saw huge fan blades being loaded

off of a ship onto trucks, one blade for each 18-wheeler trailer. To see so many huge, whirling blades at one time on a wind farm is breathtaking.

Folks have asked why we're not at the *Hope Lodge*, a free, temporary housing facilities for cancer patients who are undergoing treatment, sponsored by the American Cancer Society. We're at Staybridge Suites, a hotel chain, for two reasons. We can have Gigi and eventually Atticus here with us, they have a liberal pet policy. Also, when the kids are back from NJ we'd like to have them down on weekends to see Dad as much as possible. Those are two things we can't do at Hope Lodge *(no pets, no kids)*.

Our current hotel also has a pool, an exercise room, free laundry and each room has a small kitchenette. We're about 3/4 of a mile from Mayo and twice now we've walked home instead of taking the shuttle. Walking is good, and as Gerry recovers from the transplant – when walking is encouraged – it will be even better to have

that as an option. It was a rough choice, but seeing Gerry petting Gigi is worth so much to both of us.

I mention this because many folks have been so kind, purchasing my Red Carpet Convertible knit dress pattern and helping us out. I was chatting with another person in a similar situation to ours, someone with decent health insurance but who needs help with the extra bits *(airfare, etc.)*.

She mentioned that although she appreciates help from folks, sometimes it almost feels as though by helping they become a stockholder with a say in the financial decisions made during the health crisis.

I don't feel this way – well, not *entirely* – but I do feel a certain accountability to folks who have been so good to us. Thank you! I feel it's necessary for us to live as well and as frugally as we can, for Gerry to work hard to recover, and for us to do as much as we can to assist his recovery.

Gigi is instrumental in that. Gerry's definitely happier with a cat around. *Oh yeah, and the kids, too.*

August Fourteenth
A Weight Is Lifted
Rochester, MN

We have a new case worker with our insurance company, and we discovered something quite wonderful. We get a *[small]* daily stipend for meals and room! It's not huge, it doesn't cover everything, but it's more than we thought we'd be getting. This is amazing.

Apparently when we were looking into the program at the University of Minnesota the stipend wasn't available because Gerry would be an in-patient. When we moved our treatment to Mayo, Gerry became an outpatient and thus the stipend kicked in. But we didn't know about it, not until the *new* case worker made us aware of it.

I hadn't realized just what a weight this was on my mind until it was gone, and suddenly it's like I removed a pair of dark glasses, everything is lighter! *Actually, today everything is overcast weather-wise, and we had some major hail last night lashing at the window, but in our internal world it's sunny and bright!*

Gerry slept better last night than he has in weeks.

With all our appointments, I didn't think I'd be getting much knitting done for the first week. But I'm making progress on three separate projects and sketching as much as I can. The unique clothing pieces and beautiful artworks all around the Mayo are very inspirational.

AUGUST SIXTEENTH
ALL SYSTEMS GO!
(AN ODDLY RELIGIOUS POST…)
ROCHESTER, MN

We've been waiting for the final approval from our insurance company for Gerry's transplant. First we received a pre-approval, a guarantee that the insurance *will* cover us being here for testing and all of the preliminary stuff. After the testing is turned in and reviewed by the insurance company, then they either approve or reject the actual procedure.

It's a frustration. Obviously Gerry *needs* this, but we've been feeling as if we're waiting for someone in a cubicle to give a thumbs up. In our case, our insurance company seemed oddly concerned with *certain* samples. When these were finally turned in there was a several-day delay, hand wringing, and as of last night we still hadn't received approval.

Gerry's been scheduled to start *today*, so it was with great relief that we heard from insurance early this morning that we're good to go. Huzzah!

Today Gerry had his first Growth Hormone shot. These do several things; they make the body produce more stem cells *(they're looking for a total harvest of 12 million, but they'll settle for 10)* and they make the bones grow, causing pain in the joints.

The pain's been described to us as ranging from severe, *"I thought I'd go nuts!"* to mild, *"I hardly noticed, I just took a Tylenol."* Every person is different.

Gerry's already on Oxycontin and Hydrocodone for his many bone fractures, so they may just increase the dosage for breakthrough pain.

Wednesday we had a day off so Gerry and I drove up to Lake City and had dinner at a very nice restaurant on the lake. Our waitress was wearing one of the Lance Armstrong *Live Strong* bracelets and we began chatting. Her son is at the Mayo right now, in his third year of treatment for lung cancer. We had the feeling that his outlook wasn't bright.

Cancer is profound. Or, rather, the way that cancer – any earth shaking, life affecting experience – allows folks to open up to each other and understand what's *really* important, is profound.

As we chatted with this woman, we felt we'd been lightly adopted. She took extra pains with Gerry's meal *(he ordered the Bison, and loved it!)* and several times we all barely escaped tears. She told us she has ten kids. *Now 12?*

She said she'd add Gerry to her prayer list, which was lovely of her *(there was an off-duty priest sitting behind us, we were well covered)* and it made me ponder something that's been rolling around in my head.

No matter how we view our own spirituality – whether we're born-again Fundamentalist, Agnostic, Jewish, Hindu, Muslim, Atheist, traditional Catholics, laid-back Protestant or Wiccan – anything, really – we appreciate the connection that we make to something greater through meditation or prayer. That something greater could be inside us, or outside – after all, *Heaven is within us.*

At first when folks wrote to tell us their church group was praying for Gerry, I wasn't sure how to respond. We have a Jewish home, I was raised somewhere between Presbyterian and Free Methodist, and have developed *(what else?)* unorthodox ideas about the concept of god.

So usually I just write *"Thank you!"* and some version of, *"Right back at ya!"* But I do want folks to know that no matter where their good thoughts are coming from, we're happy to have them. My personal belief is that they – the good wishes – all spring from the same place.

A dear friend from back home wrote me the loveliest note a few weeks ago with this tidbit:

> *In Hinduism, there is a goddess called Durga. She is the goddess of strength and power and has ten hands (each with a special weapon from other gods) with which she single-handedly kills the most powerful demon that had attacked our planet. She is also a loving wife and caretaker of her family.*
>
> *I wish you the strength of Durga as you chart your course through this difficult time in your lives. May she give you the strength to overcome your difficulties and may Kali protect you and remove the hurdles in your path.*

Which is about the nicest thing anyone's ever wished for me – for us.

A local knitter and glassworker who invited me to her local knitting group last night created a lovely bead shaped like a bone and inscribed – in glass – with the word, *Hope*. I just love it. *She also made one for Gerry and Hannah, we're all very full of hope.*

Driving back to Rochester on 58, south of Red Wing, we passed a beautiful corn field, plowed and planted like a giant wave.

We stopped and I got out of the car to get a better look. As I turned back I was startled to see Gerry's head sticking out of the sun roof.

This is the Gerry I fell in love with – it's good to see him again! *Thank Durga!*

AUGUST SIXTEENTH
RAINY AFTERNOON
ROCHESTER, MN

The weather is working for us – albeit, not for everyone else in the county – but for us, this has been a good rainy weather weekend. When the weather's nice Gerry itches to get out and *do* something, rain is a respite!

It's overcast, grey, sleep-all-afternoon-while--watching-history-documentaries kind of weather. Gerry's feeling the effects from his growth hormone shots; achy joints, general malaise and tiredness, but *no* fever so far. Yay! Tonight at 5:00 p.m. we call the hospital to get the results from Gerry's blood test. If the numbers are good, we start the harvest tomorrow. If the numbers aren't where we'd like, we have another day of growth hormone shots.

The nurse who gave Gerry his growth injections on Friday and Saturday looked like Vincent D'onofrio in scrubs, and had a nice sense of humor. I gave him a flip knit book and it made him laugh. The nurse who reviewed the harvesting procedure with us on Thursday passed along one of my flip books to a knitter on staff, who emailed me to welcome us to Rochester. We'll have *everyone* on our BMT *(blood marrow transplant)* team knitting by the time I leave!

Gerry's editing some video that we shot on Friday; he told me that he looks so old when he sees himself move on tape. He worries that he'll never be able to stand up straight again. We're wondering exactly how much of the bone damage to his back is irreversible. We were able to get a board between the mattress and springs, which makes everything more comfortable for G, and we'll have ourselves cuddled today for an afternoon of rest. *History of Britain, all 15 episodes, here we come!*

I'm putting the finishing touches on an interfaith essay that's due tomorrow. I try to write from outside myself – disinterestedly? – when I write about interfaith issues.

Sometimes writing about writing is the kiss of death, that whole brain-getting-in-the-way thing that I talk about in my classes. Our brains are so powerful that we can stymie ourselves when we try to rein our brains into one specific direction. Especially when we're just at the point of a huge leap, but fearfully stop ourselves, which can make us crash.

I've come to believe that intuition is earned, bit by bit, through a lifetime of experience, observation and reflection. It's the power to take the reins from the brain so that we're not trying to quantify every tiny thing as we process it. It's accepting our own natural brilliance and letting ourselves trust our brains to know where they're going. *Easier said than done.*

So my in-the-zone method of writing about something so personal as my own spiritual journey is an attempt to find an intuitive way to explain one woman's walk in the general direction of Judaism. Of course, I equate everything with knitting, which I see as a complement to every facet of my life.

August Nineteenth
Clever Little Cells
Rochester, MN

We heard this evening that Gerry's blood count is good enough to start the harvest tomorrow – hooray! We're glad to be moving on to the next level of this adventure. I swear, it's like a video game.

This makes us oddly giddy, as if Gerry's done something very smart with his little cells *(and he has)*. So tomorrow at 7:00 a.m. we'll be at the Gonda building with bells on, and they'll start the harvesting, separating the stem cells from other blood cells and returning the blood cells to Gerry.

We'll have a threshing party and we'll hope for the best! *Harvest is always such a busy time!*

Gerry and I went to dinner the other night and the waitress told us it was Happy Hour.

When she walked away Gerry said, *sotto voce* and in mock indignation, *"Happy Hour? I'm not happy. I have cancer. When are they going to have <u>cancer</u> hour?"*

We got a funny email from the family that's watching Max in NJ. To deal with the lice they've covered his head in mayonnaise and as they were putting him to bed they told him, *"Hey Max, now <u>you're</u> at the mayo Clinic, too!"*

August Twentieth
Fourteen Years
Rochester, MN

Today is part one of the two-day celebration that is our Wedding Anniversary. Gerry and I were married by a judge on Friday, August 20, 1993. Then on Saturday we had a larger non-religious ceremony for family and friends. Fourteen years ago today.

The traditional gift for a 14th anniversary is ivory or an elephant related gift. I got Gerry a refurbished iPod. It's black, but it has white earbuds *(almost ivory?)*.

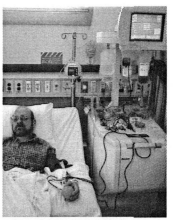

He's been listening to Confessions of an Economic Hitman during his five-hour stem cell harvesting session today. I can tell it's wearing him out, but so far he's not suffering the side effects they've mentioned – tingly fingers or nose and nausea. Our big celebration today will be returning to the hotel and putting Gerry to bed with a nice grilled chicken breast. I'm going to see if it's okay if he has a little champagne. Or beer.

Currently there's some serious flooding in Southeast Minnesota, but it feels like it's happening on another planet, we're so engrossed in Gerry's own drama. As we were leaving the Gonda building, the music of choice today was *"Seasons in the Sun."* I walked all the way to the car and had the walker and our various bags half packed up before I realized what I was humming.

"We had joy, we had fun..."

August Twenty-Second
Wheat & Chaff
Rochester, MN

Gerry had his third day of cell harvesting today, and it's been a bumper crop! So far they're obtaining a lot of cells from his collection – almost 9 million in three days (1.3 million on day one, 3.1 million on day two and 4.4 million on day three). Harvesting in Minnesota, and just in time for the State Fair!

The SHARPLES SEPARATOR COMPANY
Builders of Tubular Separators
WEST CHESTER PENNSYLVANIA

We had a bunch of news today. All of the health- –related news was good, and all of the other type of news not so good. But not so bad, just not great. News, good, bad or indifferent, can be overwhelming when it all comes at once.

The hard part is separating the good from the bad – the wheat from the chaff. Good thing we have a separator.

Gerry will have a central line for the chemo and infusion, but they prefer to collect his cells though an arm vein if possible. Central lines = possibility of complication.

Gerry has "good" veins, so this means that each day of harvest starts with some painful poking, but a complication would be more painful!

We're hopeful that Gerry'll have a relatively short time with those awful long needles up his veins. If he does this well tomorrow then we'll have our full collection. *Then we can perform the traditional stem cell harvest dance!*

Gerry's using his own stem cells, they're the best match for him. They'll *"scrub"* them to get rid of as many plasma cells *(the potential cancer cells)* as they can. The chemo should take care of most of the plasma cells in his body. Then his scrubbed stem cells will be infused back into his veins where they will go into his bone marrow and – hopefully – start making new stem cell babies.

I went out again to the weekly knitting group that's adopted me here in Rochester. I feel at home with these women, they're kind and lots of fun!

On the way I picked up a friend I'd met in the harvesting ward, a lovely woman *(and knitter)* who is here with her husband, also undergoing a BMT for MM. It was fun to introduce her to my new knitting and coffee friends. I love seeing nice folks network and meet each other. And, like me, I knew she could use a break from hospitals and cancer related talk.

On the drive there we chatted about how much we love our husbands but how frustrated we can get. I showed her the cliff I threaten to toss Gerry off of every now and then. The things that wives of cancer patients can only share with each other. *Don't tell anyone, okay?*

I also got a not-so-great phone call today. Apparently during one of Hannah's sleepover sessions with her friends back in New Jersey, a whole bunch of little "friends" decided to nest in her hair. *Well, hers and everyone else's, too.*

If you don't have kids, you may be grossed out by this, but if you do have kids you'll realize that it's become more common to find outbreaks of lice every now and then. *Ick*. So Hannah is staying with the kindest family in the world – folks who weren't even involved in any of this outbreak stuff – and they've agree to let her stay

153

with them for another week so that she doesn't have to fly with this contagion or share it with her cousins in Boston.

Hannah's sad not to be seeing her cousin, but thrilled to be able to spend more time with her best friends back in NJ. After an hour on the phone with two different folks at Continental, it's all squared away.

As soon as I hung up the hotel phone, our cell phone rang and – *guess what?*

Yep, Maxie has the "L" word.

AUGUST TWENTY-FIFTH
IN THE RIGHT PLACE
ROCHESTER, MN

I am so happy. I feel so lucky – fortunate, blessed, whatever the word you want to use – that we ended up here for this period in our lives.

So, whether my standing half-joke that my mother and brother were yelling at me from the great beyond to *"Move your family to Minneosta!"* is true, or whether we just got lucky enough to find a home a mere 81 miles from the pre-eminent research center for Multiple Myeloma, we're in a *good* place.

Gerry was getting a bit of a swelled head with his monumental collections of stem cells, so on Thursday the stem cell gods had to take him down a peg. Mayo was only able to collect enough cells to bring him up to 10.8 million, so we had to go in again on Friday. It was a bummer to him that he had to get back in that bed and lay for 5 hours, but now we're WAY over the hoped-for goal of 12 million cells. We are the proud owners of

13,110,000 cells and we have plenty for future stem cell transplants if/when that need arises.

When Gerry was finished around 1:00 p.m. we hugged everyone, I passed out some books and signed them for the many knitting nurses. We hopped in the car and drove up to pick up Atticus, then continued to Minneapolis for a fund raiser I was doing at the Textile Center. It was a blast to have Gerry and Atticus with me for my book-signing talk. Gerry had never heard me do my *"thing"* before – *neither had Atticus* – so it was a little nerve-wracking.

My talk was well received, folks laughed and I used the poor guy in the front row, husband of a knitter, as a foil for a lot of jokes. He took it very well, he was a *mensch*. He laughed a lot, which made me feel exceptionally happy because sometimes I'm afraid a lot of my humorous stuff may be too knitter-specific.

But, even though I scooted around my topic from 14 different directions, I came out at the right place. There's a formula, famously ridiculed in the Woody Allen film *Crimes and Misdemeanors:*

$$Tragedy + Time = Comedy$$

I realized last night that the point of my whole teaching – my whole knitting career – is this formula:

$$Mistakes + Grace = Wisdom$$

Last night on the drive home from my lecture at the Textile Center we took a detour so we could enjoy the downtown Minneapolis skyline. I could tell that Gerry felt calmer and happier than he has in a long time.

August Twenty-Seventh
Today Sucked
Rochester, MN

Yes, it did.

Today we moved into a new, larger room because Gerry's mom is coming to stay here with him. *Is there any way I can explain how sick I am of moving?*

Every time I turn around there's another room full of furniture, suitcases, boxes that has to be moved to *another* room. As the functioning, strong-as-bull adult, the task falls to me. I'm tired and worn out, both mentally and physically. Emotionally I'm *just* holding my own.

Unfortunately, the Wifi doesn't work well in our new room. When I called the desk for help the resident handyman/I.T. guy came to our room, but he wasn't terribly helpful. He was also more than a little condescending. *("You're on a Mac? Oh, well, lady that's the problem...")*

Ooooh, I was so mad. Obviously the power outage caused by the thunder storm last night affected their router, so how about resetting the modem, genius? *Yes, I can be condescending, too.*

Since I was so tired, we figured we'd eat out. On the way to dinner I ran over an already dead deer that was lying in the road. I was able to straddle it under our car, so I don't think it did any damage, but it was exciting. I couldn't avoid it, there was a car in the lane next to me and it just *appeared* as I came over a hill. *I envisioned the condescending handyman.*

At dinner I choked, to the amusement of the table next to us, who didn't realize I was really in trouble and thought I was goofing. I retched *(no one laughed at that!)* and it took me a good 30 minutes for my throat to "calm down." Scary.

Or maybe just a pathetic bid for attention after the deer incident garnered too-little sympathy from Gerry?

Can running over a deer cause dysphagia?

August Thirty-First
Second Honeymoon (with Chemo...)
Rochester, MN

The past few weeks have been a very special time. Being able to be alone with Gerry – well, except for the doctors and nurses doing intimate things with G that I won't even go into – has been a tremendous experience. We've had such a good time, *which isn't how Cancer is supposed to be, right?*

We've been sightseeing, taking odd drives to figure out exactly *what* those smokestacks in the distance are, and I've been going on daily walks with Atticus around the church at St. Mary's Hospital. It's lovely.

We've enjoyed each other's company, and after 14 years of marriage we both feel pretty lucky that it's been such a great few weeks. We laugh all the time, at the stupidest things, and have a good time with just about everything we do. As Zero Day approaches we've been getting a bit more tense, but nothing we can't handle.

And now, tomorrow – er, today – is Zero Day. This is the day of the transplant, which is supposed to be anticlimactic after all of the bizarre things that have transpired to this point. Every day after this is numbered Zero Day Plus One, Zero Day Plus Two, etc.

At Day Plus One Hundred we're supposed to come back to Mayo for follow-up. The nurse practitioner told us Thursday that when someone lives as close as we do, they tend to let them head home sooner than someone who lives halfway around the world. She actually used the words, *"Day Plus Fifteen"* when making an educated guess on when Gerry might be able to go home.

Because the transplant is today, the last day of August, counting the days for the first month will be quite easy. Day Plus 1 is Sept 1, Day Plus 15 is Sept 15. And that's the day I'm returning from *[gleam]* France.

Everything, though, seems to be coming together beautifully. Gerry had his second day of chemo yesterday and so far so good. He's not supposed to feel the effects for five days or so – when I'll be in *[gleam]* France. Gerry's mom and sister arrived Wednesday without a hitch. The kids arrived and they're beautiful, healthy, happy and lice-free! *Thank you kind Devi, Alison and Andrea for the hours of treating our kids!*

We have all of his meds sorted out for his mom in a compartmentalized container. We're getting the sterile room routine down.

Back in St. Paul the bathroom floor is laid, *it's lovely.* The kitchen floor should be down on Friday so the new bathroom is almost entirely finished. Oh, and I'm leaving on Sunday evening for *[gleam]* France. *Bonjour!* And the inn I'm staying at has Wifi.

Gerry is doing really well. He's still basking in the 13,000,000 plus stem cell harvest *(I'm going to have a T-shirt made up for him touting this amazing feat)*, and he wanted to walk to the clinic for his second day of chemo, except we were running late. *Darn.* Our [fabulous] nurses yesterday told us that every day that he's able to be active and move around means 5 fewer days of recovery down the road. So as long as he feels like it, we'll walk. Plus, it's been a beautiful few days here in Rochester, sunny and cool, perfect for walking half a mile!

Gerry told me yesterday that the night before, the night when he couldn't get to sleep until 4:00 a.m., he seriously thought about death for the first time.

We didn't talk about it in depth, but with all of our joking about *"Hey, the service here is terrible! I don't have much time, you know!"* this was the first time the hooded one entered the room for anything but a chuckle *(or a game of Battleship or Twister...).*

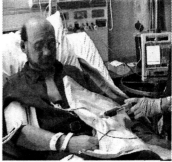

AUGUST THIRTY-FIRST

POST TRANSPLANT UPDATE

ROCHESTER, MN

The 5:45 a.m. appointment with surgery for Gerry's central line went very smoothly. The line is in, I've changed the dressing once (I watched the video *twice* before I did it), and it seems to be healing beautifully.

Our amazing Gerry, everything his body's been asked to do has been done magnificently. The chemo was put in through Gerry's central line, he felt great, the nurses were wonderful *(as usual here at Mayo)*, and we're getting so used to feeling lucky we don't know what we'll do when we have to go back to feeling like *"normal people."*

It's kind of a crappy way to feel special, but better to embrace the positive aspect of this whole adventure, *ne c'est pas?* Hey, that's *French!*

I've missed several design submission deadlines, I've done _no_ work on any book proposals and I've barely been able to get any knitting done at all this week. I'm planning on getting a lot done on the flights from Minnesota to London, then from London to _[gleam]_ France, but I need to double- and triple-check the needle allowances on international flights.

Since I'm working on a mitered project I can use short double pointed needles, so I may just bring them and pack everything else in my luggage to be safe. They're slower than my long metal needles, but I'd hate to lose my best tools to TSA!

And me? I'm tired, but good. Lots of work yet to be done, much more behind me. When I stop and think about the work it overwhelms me, so instead I just make sure the next few days are planned out and put one foot in front of the other.

Today my sister-in-law Gayle and I drove up to St. Paul to clean the house and pick up the kids. The house is _far_ from pristine, but it's light years better than it was! Our ten-plus-year-old vacuum cleaner, which was a cheapo stopgap when we bought it and has never been great, was just too lightweight for the massive task. So I stopped at Sears on the way to St. Paul and finally got myself a halfway decent true HEPA vacuum.

Armed with our new vacuum and face masks, we cleaned like there was no tomorrow. Gayle worked so hard, and at the end of three hours 90% of the dust was gone, things were in a better working order, and we felt quite pleased with ourselves. Saturday Gayle, the kids and I will drive up and I'll get them settled in before I leave Sunday afternoon for – oh, _you know_...

I knew this would be a lot of work, but I hadn't realized how MUCH work. Every single minute is devoted to either lifting, carrying, arranging, cleaning, phoning, picking up or dropping off. It is very much like having a baby or toddler (a very *large* toddler) who has definite opinions about certain things, and also a certain amount of pride.

Gerry's been amazing, just wonderful, and I am very lucky. I can imagine how easily this could disintegrate into something very unpleasant if either caregiver or patient lacked respect for what the other was going through. Gerry appreciates all that I'm doing, and that means so much. On my end, I never lose sight of how hard and odd this whole thing is for Gerry, who up until six months ago felt pretty darned good.

But even as great as Gerry's been, because he IS an adult human, I can't just steamroll him and push him along. He has pride and an ego (as we all do), and he needs to be able to make as many decisions for himself as he can. *This would be easy if it were a dictatorship – as long as I were the dictator.*

Sometimes, in addition to all the other work, I find myself cajoling, wheedling, and pulling him toward a decision or choice. Not that Gerry's being recalcitrant, just *human.* And I know in my heart of hearts that I'd be 1000% times more difficult. *Actually, I have been 1000% more difficult, so Gerry has a long way to go before I have anything to complain about!*

Gerry mentioned the other day I haven't been talking much about France, so I bought a guidebook for Languedoc and I'm trying to drum up the enthusiasm that this trip deserves. My heart is wrenched with the thought that when Gerry's at his absolute worst, I'll be resting pool side in Southern France.

September

It's done. Gerry's at the top of the first hill in his roller coaster and is about to go shooting down into the valley.

Right now his blood counts are good and his appetite is good. And – aside from the overwhelming odor of stale, rotten, vinegary creamed corn emanating from his body due to the preservative used with the stem cells – he's pretty normal. But we're told that will change in the next few days. By day Plus Five or Plus Six, his counts will be low, and he'll be *lower*.

It will be rough, so they say, and I won't be there to make him feel better. I'll be in France. No gleam this time. I'll be feeling like a happy, relaxed piece of *merde*.

My sister-in-law and I drove up to St. Paul today with the kids, dog and cat, and moved ourselves back into the house. The kitchen's looking good, another few days and the floor will be entirely down. By the end of the week the cabinets are supposed to be in, then the appliances go in. But it means that Gayle and the kids will be without a kitchen.

When we arrived there was a *huge* amount of cleaning to do in the basement, sweeping, dusting and mopping. We had to light the pilot light for the water heater, I really need a shower! My work still isn't finished, but I pooped out and said we should stop and go to dinner.

Returning to a dark house we suddenly realized that large portions of our home are lacking electricity. This means a big, heavy duty orange extension cord is now running up to the second floor with smaller cords branching off to the bedrooms providing one light and one fan per room. This involved a lot of running around and pushing furniture in the darkening, hot house – and a lot of swearing.

But we finally have a relatively cool and light house. I hate leaving things in this state for my sister-in-law. She is a saint. A *mensch-ette*, n'est ce pas?

SEPTEMBER THIRD

JE SUIS ARRIVEÉ!

FAUGÈRES, FRANCE

En Francais, s'il vous plaid! I know, I'm probably all screwed up with my French. *[Galic shrug] Eh...*

Everything went so smoothly yesterday that I felt as if I must be dreaming. Bags packed, able to log onto the computer in the house and print out my boarding pass, the drive to the airport was very quick, and check in was easy. I changed $100 into Euros. Woo!

Then I boarded and settled in, not even needing to use the bathroom during the flight (a first for me). I got some nice shots of Greenland as we flew over. We arrived in London a little after 8:00 a.m., circling over the green, countryside, beautiful in the summer morning light.

Apparently they believe in the power of walking at Gatwick airport. It felt like a five mile hike from the gate to the bus to take me to the other terminal. Then another hike to get my boarding pass, and yet another 15 minute hike to the gate.

They made me check one of my carry-on bags, and that piece of luggage has now been lost. It's *supposed* to show up tomorrow, but it's an hour drive from the airport in Montpellier to our inn. In the whole scheme of things-that-could-have-gone-wrong, though, the whole flight went pretty darned well!

And it's my birthday! I'm 46.

Several officials have checked my passport today, but no congratulations. C'est dommage. The drive to La Vigneronne, our inn, was lovely! I hadn't expected the

landscape to remind me so much of the area east of San Diego. I've never been this far south in France, and it was hotter than I'd thought it would be. *Well, what did I expect? I'm at the Mediter-frickin'-anean Sea!*

After arriving I to the pool for a quick swim to cool off, then back to my room for a nice nap, then down to dinner. This is living.

My favorite part of the delicious dinner? The baked chevre and greens salad! Now I'm back in my lovely attic room, quite romantic. Except for the wifi, it could be any year between 850 and 1600 c.e.

I have the same trepidation I always have the night before I'm starting a new class. I've asked everyone to think of something they'd like to learn, so they get to do something they want. *And they'll have as much Annie-time as they can stomach.*

I'm so darned tired with the jet lag, wine and all the running up and down stairs that I'm not sure if I'll stay awake for my shower. *How embarrassing it would be to fall asleep under the running water!*

SEPTEMBER FOURTH

LA VIGNERONNE

FAUGÈRES, FRANCE

The class today went very well. It's funny how much I worry about these classes. Well, perhaps not *worry*, but how deep the concern runs until I get going and get a handle on what type of students I have.

In this case, the students are quite wonderful! Since many of the tour are shop owners, they definitely know their way around a knitting needle.

This morning we did some Combination Knitting and ended with Cables. This is sort of a mainstay for me, and a good way to quickly get to know the students, how they knit, how adventurous or quietly competent they are. This is a wonderful class. So fun, so diverse, yet all so open to new things and great conversation. *Perhaps the wine helps...?*

The food has been absolutely amazing. Simple, traditional country French, well-prepared, delicious! I'm not a foodie, I don't cook a lot, but I love good food. I don't know as much about it as I hope to some day, but that doesn't prevent me from thoroughly enjoying these lovely meals!

One thing I *do* know is that this is the best food I've had in my life. Delicious and satisfying, excellent wine, amazing desserts. *C'est parfait!* And the more I drink, the better my French gets!

Gerry and I have been able to email back and forth, thank heaven! He told me that Monday he had to have two pints of blood in a transfusion because his hemoglobin levels were low. This is not unexpected, but, of course, I hate be away. Okay, not *hate*. I'm having an amazing time here.

He and his mom have been walking between the clinic and hotel as much as possible, which is wonderful for both of them. The more he walks, the faster his recovery and the stronger his lungs remain. Plus it gets them out, gives them something to do, and allows them to enjoy the fresh air every day.

I get a feeling that the boredom is almost as debilitating as the nausea.

September Sixth
The Miracle of Mirth
Faugères, France

I've seldom laughed more than I have in the past few days. This, in addition to seeing so many beautiful places, experiencing so many exceptional wines, and enjoying foods I'd never dreamed I'd be eating, makes me wonder why it took so long to return to France.

When Gerry is troubled because the kids are finicky eaters, I look down guiltily because I was, and remain, a bit of a finicky eater. There are things I just don't like (tomatoes) and after a yearly ritual of trying them, I've given up.

But this week I'm learning that it's silly to give up. And I'm trying all kinds of new food. Maybe not tomatoes, but I did try a few other things these past days – and I'm very glad I did!

While the rest of the group shopped in Pezenas, I stayed behind to rest a bit and try to catch up on email. After my *"office work"* was done, I sat downstairs waiting for Phil to come and pick me up, loving the wind and the sun and the dancing plane trees. These lovely trees line roads, canals, walkways, all over this region. At times the proximity of the trees to the road makes driving tight, so we've heard there are some major accidents.

There seems to be a movement afoot to cut them down, and a counter movement to let them be. They've obviously been around longer than the cars have, and it would be a terrible loss to cut them down so folks can drive like idiots. *They'd just find a stone wall to crash against, anyway...*

Dinner was absolutely stunning. The food was *nouveau*, trendy, *trés chic*, but not over-the-top and silly. Translating the descriptions of the desserts, though, taxed the full bi-lingual skills of both Kris, one of the tour hostesses and our waiter. Kris and her husband, Phil, have devised a whole series of these tours under the name of her company, French Girl Knits.

French folks eat later than we do, and it's been hard for the group to get used to that. We go so long between meals that – however good the food is – there's that low blood sugar period when it's rough to keep going. By the time our late supper ended many of us were just *wiped out!* It was a quiet ride back to the inn

Kris and Phil are taking steps to help us over this difficulty. I purchased some cookies at a local supermarket to offer during my class *(if I don't eat them all)* to keep my students at an even keel between the amazing meals!

SEPTEMBER SIXTH

TRAVAIL DIFFICILE

FAUGÈRES, FRANCE

After a lace class this morning, where I forced everyone to work harder than they'd expected *(I've learned the French word for "yell" and I'm looking up "whip"),* we took off for the Patchwork Museum in Sallèles d'Aude — a beautiful spot with ducks!

Marie, the proprietress, made us at home as we shared a picnic lunch that Regine at La Vingeronne put together. So beautiful, so simple, and so *good!* The goat cheese here is exceptional, and I actually ate Boar Pâté and Blood Cheese. *To think that I once quailed at stuffed derma.*

After a lovely and restful hour of sitting and knitting and looking through the gallery, we headed off to Beziers for dinner, stopping along the way at a

169

supermarket *(I have to admit, I was the instigator of that detour...)* to pick up stuff we all needed.

Lisa – one of my new friends – needed to download images from her camera onto a disk to clear space so she could take more photographs. I am not sure how I did it, but I walked into a photo shop, explained the situation, got a price for the job and a time when the disk would be ready – all *en Français*! I was SO pumped!

We shopped, bought some T-shirts, soaps, cookies, one of our number bought a curling iron, much needed toothpaste, and then we checked ourselves out using the self serve kiosk. It was less exciting than we'd hoped because English was an option – *c'est dommage*! I'd been dealing with an off-and-on headache, so I stopped at a pharmacy and, once again in iffy French, I asked for medicine for a very strong headache, asked the price of some other stuff and bought shower gel. I am *golden*.

I know it's a little pathetic, how impressed I am with myself, but I was walking on air!

Dinner was magnificent with a salad that was, hands down, the best I've ever had in my life. And – *tada* – I actually ate *paté*. Yes, I understand all the horrible things that they do to the geese. *(A running joke through this trip, every time we eat a wonderful piece of meat, is that they have very happy pigs, cows, etc. over here in this region...)*

I'd never liked *paté* – it always had an aftertaste and I just hated it. But *this*, I loved!

On Thursday while everyone else took off for a day trip by the Spanish border, I stayed at La Vingeronne and slept in until 11:30 a.m. As I'd missed *petit dejuner* I took a hike up the big hill to a restaurant and had a wonderful meal that I could *not* finish. I said *"Non"* to dessert. Alert the media.

I hiked back down the hill, stopping for some knitting on a bench at a lovely spot, and wandered through the tiny old town of Faugères. There's a 15th Century windmill up on the hill, and I almost hiked up to that, but I changed my mind and returned to the inn, ostensibly to knit, but guess what I did? *Napped.*

I took a shower, washed out my personal items, put on some music and laid down for five minutes. It turned into a two-and-a-half hour nap, and I feel like a new woman.

I can hear that the group has returned – and it's 7:30 p.m. so dinner should be soon! Another dinner at La Vigneronne – how lucky can we be?

VITE!

FAUGÈRES, FRANCE

So who should show up on Thursday but the Fastest Knitter In The World? It was such a delight to actually meet Miriam Tegels in person. We've been emailing for a few years, and she's just as kind and lovely in person as she is in her emails!

We spent a lot of time together over the next two days and everyone *so* enjoyed watching her knit.

I wasn't even going to try to knit up to her speed, I know when discretion is appropriate, and I'd rather look discrete than slow-as-a-snail!

Mostly I just enjoyed walking around with Miriam. She's a delightful friend, and we had a lovely coffee while we both knitted. How good to spend time with a sister knitter with whom I didn't have to be *"teacher"* - just Annie.

I love everyone on the tour, but I was able to feel a little less *"on"* than I had the previous few days. It was also nice for me watch someone else knit just for pure pleasure for a change!

At the market I bought a sweater for 5 euros, I could tell that Miriam was vaguely scandalized that I don't knit all my own stuff. I wish I had time! My project is going slower than I'd anticipated and I'm kicking myself for not thinking to hire Miriam knit it for me. *Merde*!

Today we went to the seaside and ate oysters and amazingly sweet shrimp for lunch, then we took the tram into Montpellier and walked and shopped for a bit. Our dinner was in a former bath (*bain*) and it was quite beautiful! We ate in a courtyard covered with umbrellas, the food was exquisite (best dessert so far – Symphony of *Creme Brulée*!), and we laughed and laughed.

At one point I began speaking with one of the women in the group who has become very dear to me, and the subject turned to our husbands. It's probably the excess of wine and the time away from Gerry, but I had to go to the bathroom for a moment to collect myself. *Where is my PT Cruiser when I need it?*

Saturday was market day in Pézenas, where we went for some more shopping and a fine lunch. And I ate olives. Today I moved into a different room with a dresser, larger bed and window, a private toilette and shower, a small desk and places to sit. I'm in heaven!

Most important, I'm one floor above the teaching area, so I won't have to go halfway around the building and up three steep flights of stairs to grab that ball of yarn or book I left in my room.

You'd think I'd be thinner after all the walking and stair climbing, but it seems the wine and amazing food has taken care of that! It was romantic to be in a "garret" but I did look forward to a room with a bit more comfort and fewer stairs.

Saturday the tour guests left, most of them at 6:30 this morning. I really love the time to myself. And in some ways I am overcome with the feeling that this is sort of training wheels for a period when I will be more alone. *Geeze, is it me, or is it the wine that's making me so darned maudlin?*

I'm constantly thinking, *"How much more fun this would be if Gerry were here!"* He makes me laugh more than anyone else in the world, I need that when I'm spending so much time making other people laugh!

I don't think he's in a laughing mood right now, though. He's sick as a *chien* and this weekend his platelet count was low. Right now he's fighting a fever.

His sister and mom both have the number of the inn and will call me if he wants or needs to speak with me. I hate to call and bother him at a time when he may finally be resting.

SEPTEMBER THIRTEENTH
SPACES BETWEEN POSTS
FAUGÈRES, FRANCE

I miss my several-times-a-week catching up on what is on my mind, and feel as though the past two weeks have been more a travelogue of my trip in France than musings on a hand knit designer's life.

But life is what it is, and right now a large part of mine is traveling by van all over Languedoc, France.

The new group arrived on Monday afternoon, Tuesday we had our first class then went into town for some shopping. Cats were befriended and gelato was eaten. Wednesday afternoon we went off to the Patchwork Museum again, but instead of taking the tour this time I walked around the canal and enjoyed some solitude.

I watched the locks filling with water to transport a boat from the shallow end to the high end – fascinating – I couldn't help but wish that Maxie were here to see it!

I'm finding that I require more time alone this week, which is most likely due to the fact I'm at the end of a two week stint away from Gerry and the kids. But it's necessary, so I'm grabbing what I can.

Speaking of Gerry, at the Patchwork Museum one of the students let me use her cell phone (my own isn't working here) and I was able to speak with him! He sounded very good, and apparently after a very hard week his blood numbers are on the rise and every day is a little better. He mentioned that he's losing his facial hair, so I'm wondering what I'll see by the time I get home!

Then back home to La Vingerone before rising this morning for a drive down to Collioure near the Spanish border. Collioure is an amazingly beautiful town on the Mediterranean. We broke into smaller groups and wandered the streets, I settled at a sidewalk cafe and just knit for several hours.

The sheer volume of Gelato establishments in Collioure is breathtaking, I don't know how I managed to stop at only one. The flavors were excellent, but nothing like the *marron glaceé* that our hosts at La Vignerone provided

for dessert this evening. Amazing! They have *marron* spread that I must get before I leave!

I'm scheduled to leave on Saturday morning, so tomorrow is my last full day here. I hope that class goes well, there's so much I'd still like to show the students! And then off for a final bit of shopping, finding gifts for folks back home who have done so much for us lately.

This has been an extraordinary trip, an amazing opportunity, and I hope that I've experienced it as fully as I could. This past week, missing Gerry, was more of a challenge than I had thought it would be, but we only grow when we're challenged so I'm glad for the opportunity.

I'm looking forward to seeing the kids and Gerry *(and Atticus and Gigi)*, but I'm also very excited about having the distance to reflect on this trip. Time and distance will let me do a post mortem on my teaching, the classes I offered and how it may have been done better. I can't decide if wine helps or if it just makes it worse.

September Sixteenth
Beauty & Home
St. Paul, MN

My last few days in France were very beautiful! The weather was excellent (just enough of a nip to make

walking comfortable), the wine was plentiful and the company was a lot of fun. And then there's the scenery...

We went into Montpellier on Friday. I'd been feeling like an evening walk, so while the others went to the restaurant, I strolled around Montpellier, soaking in the elegant architecture and amazing sunset. I don't know if it was just me, or the knowledge that it was my final evening in southern France after two very full weeks, but the sky seemed much more beautiful than it had before. I walked for quite a bit, seeing wonderful sights like the Domino Pizza guy on a scooter.

Even though I knew I'd be joining the group at the restaurant for dessert *(Symphony of Crème Brulée!)*, I was drawn to a Lebanese restaurant for an almond pastry. And, yes, it was delicious. *Eh, what the hell — my last night, right?*

At the restaurant our group finished very late, though, and I began obsessing about the long tram ride/drive back to the inn and my LONG flight the next day.

But, of course, I had packing to do, and goodbyes to say, and I stayed up waaay too late. I figured I'd sleep on the plane.

The change at Gatwick was hell, but I knew that going in. I literally *ran* from one plane to the shuttle bus, then *ran* from the shuttle bus to the check-in desk only to be told – snottily – *"Well, we're running rather late, aren't we?"* Stuck up wench.

I told her I didn't know about *late*, but I was certainly *running*. Damn that Lebanese almond pastry.

It was exciting to fly over snowy Greenland. Many folks on the plane were drawn to the windows *(I figured they were homesick Minnesotans)*, but I had an eagle-eye view from my seat. Nothing, however, was more beautiful than flying in over St. Paul.

And who was waiting as I scooted off the plane in record time and through customs without a hitch? My darling kiddies and my dear friend, Nancy.

She flew in from New Jersey and has been staying with the kids all week, I cannot thank her enough. The antique chemise from the Patchwork Museum is a very small way to show how grateful I am.

Today I drove down to Rochester with the kids to see Gerry. I'm still jet-lagged, so the four hours of driving there and back was mostly on coffee-pilot. Gerry surprised me with a Tom Tom GPS system *(a refurb – he knows that the best gift he can give me is a bargain!)* for my birthday. And for the first time in almost three weeks the whole family was together. I even brought down Atticus for the visit.

There is no more beautiful word in any language than *"Home."*

September Seventeenth
The Threshold
St. Paul, MN

For all of those who have been so kind to write and say, *"You're handling this with so much grace!"* maybe you don't want to read this post. Illusions are hard to see shattered.

I think today I hit the threshold. I'm hoping this is temporary – I'm sure it is – but it's not fun. My inbox has been just jammed with not just emails, but emails-which-must-be-answered. So I answer them. And then I discover that half the day is gone and I *still* have much to do.

I need to finish a *huge* project for another designer's book, the project which has taken longer than just about anything else I've ever knit. It's a huge mitered ruana. I need to finish a shawl for *VK*, due in a few days. It's a fun project, and I've been afraid to dive into the last few hours of it because I know I'll never want to return to the big mitered ruana. Mind games.

The bathroom is coming along, but we won't be ready to use it until next week. Did I mention the roots that were found in the sewer pipe last week? *How clever of me to arrange to be in France at that time.*

We're not sure when Gerry will be released, but the docs are very happy with his recovery. My big fear is that

Dining Room masquerading as Pantry & Kitchen

when he comes home with his mom the house will be unlivable; the kitchen isn't finished.

Gerry will be on antibiotics for a year, but I really don't want to tempt fate by introducing him into a dust- and construction-dirt-filled environment. We need to avoid the odd infection. *Remember the aforementioned roots in the sewer?*

I'm trying to get as much cleaned and put away as possible between knitting mitered squares for the ruana and finishing other projects. Regardless of when Gerry comes home, all of the stuff we took down to the basement will have to be moved back up to the kitchen, and that will fall to me.

We'll have the Festival of *Packing, Loading and Carrying* down in Rochester, to be followed with the Festival of *Unloading, Carrying and Unpacking* up in St. Paul.

This is in conjunction with the minor holiday known as, *"Putting All The Crap That Now Resides In The Dining Room Back In The Kitchen."*

I'm so far out of the kids' school loop, and I have to get caught up on what forms need to be returned, what homework needs to be done and signed off on, and what extra school activities must be signed up for. I just feel totally unable to make this leap right now. But I am exactly the person who needs to do it.

Most of all, though, I can't get the image of Gerry out of my head. How different he looks from just last week, and how *very* different from a few months ago. Hannah's taller than he is now; it wasn't that way when I left for France. This is the nadir, we have been told that it's all UP from here, and we're hoping that's true.

On the way to Wendy's for dinner tonight I blew a gasket because Hannah was teasing Max, Max was screaming, and Hannah wasn't letting up. *They may not do that again for a while.* Unfortunately, I've also just given them a full chapter for the tell-all book they'll write 20 years from now.

Perhaps, more than anything else, I'm missing those two bottles of wine every day that I got used to in France...?

SEPTEMBER NINETEENTH

"FANTASTIC"

ROCHESTER, MN

That was the exact quote when Dr. Hayman asked the nurse today how Gerry's recovery was going. Gerry is golden – which I've always known – and he's been an amazing overachiever in his body's stellar reaction to his chemo and transplant.

The cells are grafting, they started on Day 13 (which is supposedly a harbinger of a very good outcome), and once again I found myself weeping in a doctor's office.

Right after breakfast today Gerry called to say that his final doctor's appointment had been rescheduled for 11:00 a.m. today. I hurried on down to Rochester where Gerry, Elaine and I heard the going home instructions.

I'm leaving on Friday for a weeklong teaching trip in Northern California, and we learned yesterday that Friday is also going to be Gerry's out day. We've changed it so that he's coming home on Thursday. When things start moving, they move fast.

Gerry's Day Plus 100 appointment is scheduled at the Mayo for the second week in December. Apparently he'll be feeling light years better, his bones will be stronger, and he may even be able to straighten up when he walks if he's able to engage in physical therapy. That seems to be the main thing on his mind, getting himself back to roughly the same place he was a few months ago in his ability to walk and move.

Gerry has done as well as anyone could, his numbers are excellent, his white blood cell count is pretty amazing for someone who's gone through what he has, and he's ready to come home. Obviously bringing in the Jewish mom for the *"Eat, EAT!"* portion of the recovery was a strategic move. And how he's ready to come home.

The house is not ready, but this afternoon I engaged in an intensive scrubbing and bleaching of the basement to remove drywall dust and take care of the residual microbes left after that little sewer back up problem. I think that the house is probably as clean as it can be in the current situation. Messy, untidy, a black hole of disorganization – but clean.

SEPTEMBER TWENTIETH
Present!
ST. PAUL, MN

Everyone's in the house, and it feels so good.

But you know who seems the happiest that Dad, Mom, both kids and Grandma are all under one roof? Atticus. He's absolutely in his best element, and is so relaxed. Mr. Happy Dog.

While I was away he displayed some pretty nasty behavior. Nothing dangerous, just lots of pooping in the house, attacking backpacks, etc. Poor Nancy, it's a good thing she adores Atticus. I don't think she imagined that babysitting a nine- and ten-year-old would involve so much *poop*.

On Nancy's last night here Atticus knew she'd be leaving the next morning. He sat with his head resting on her leg all evening. He's a very perceptive dog.

I've just about had time to launder all of my stuff from France — I didn't even put it away, it goes right back into the case!

I am *very* excited about driving around a new area. I love to drive. I figured out when my mother died that *white-line meditation* works well for me.

SEPTEMBER TWENTY–FIFTH
DEPARTMENT OF LESSONS LEARNED
SACRAMENTO, CA

- *Three–star hotels charge a daily rate for internet.*
- *Two–star hotels don't.*
- *Four times out of 10, folks who are dying to ask a question aren't really interested in the answer.*
- *Subtlety is wasted on hyper-critics.*
- *Cheap shoes hurt.*
- *GPS is the best thing since sliced bread.*
- *Seven pillows can't make up for one Gerry.*

I'm able to think about things when I drive that I don't think about when I'm just sitting and knitting. I'm able to focus in a "back of the mind" way, with my most important thoughts on the guy ahead who didn't signal, or the exit I just missed. Some of my best ideas come to me when I drive, I missed not having alone driving time in August and September.

So California has been the perfect place for some hardcore driving. Not that a trip from San Mateo to Petaluma is very hardcore, but it's longer than slipping out alone to run to Target.

OCTOBER

October Fourth
New Frontier
St. Paul, MN

Today is the anniversary of Sputnik. I'm a child of the 60s – I grew up thinking it was just a matter of time until I took a stroll on the moon, and that we could do anything because we had such smart scientists in America. *And is science really that far from knitting?*

I've heard a rumor that when NASA engineers explain relatively simple procedures to each other, they say, *"After all, it's not lace knitting!"*

Lace knitting takes a fair amount of technical skill, confidence, the ability to read a pattern or follow a chart, and a desire to work to the end of a motif. I personally think our country would be a better place if one of the criteria for running for office was a demonstrable ability to knit lace.

We still have smart scientists in this country – brilliant, actually – but I feel that they're working with their hands tied. In a society where some schools teach creationism with a straight face as scientific fact, and we're not permitted to fund stem cell research with public money, science is not given the respect that it deserves. *Guns don't kill people, pipettes kill people...*

As I said to a friend a few weeks ago, *"If you're against stem cell research because you feel that you're ending a human life, do you feel that in vitro fertilization must be banned, too? Because if you're not going to stop the mechanism for creating these petrie dish punkins, then you can't really complain about stem cell research."*

I've felt this way for a long time, but it's more personal now. Gerry's stem cell transplant was via his own cells, so embryonic cells didn't enter into it.

However, research from one study has a way of enlightening other studies. I can't help but feel that, as far as we've come in treating Multiple Myeloma, we'd be further along if we'd had decent research going on in *all* areas of stem cell experimentation.

And speaking of which, Gerry continues to get better. Every day he seems a little stronger, a little more present, a little more his old self. But he's been wearing out in the afternoons and needing a nice nap. We all could use that. It's also time for us to get our flu shots.

Our biggest news is that earlier in the day Hannah and I went to the Humane Society where she picked out a little orange kitten for her birthday. Now we have two cats again, and we're very happy. She's named it Shiloh. He definitely seemed more peaceful than the Siamese cat she was thinking of getting.

I have a feeling Shiloh will end up being Gerry's cat. *Or Gerry will become Shiloh's human...*

October Seventh

Overexertion or Everyday Stress & Strain

St. Paul, MN

As we know, I've been doing a lot of lifting, carrying, moving, stretching, all kinds of putting-the-house--back-together stuff that begins to wear on a person. I used to have a bad back problem, sciatica to be exact, which I developed in grad school. All of that drafting *(by hand).*

But when I had my kids the sciatica seemed to recede into the background, and I hadn't had a bad attack for almost nine years.

Did I say background?

Friday night as I bent down to pour some seltzer, my back went, *"Pop!"* so loudly I was surprised no one else could hear it. I knew exactly what it was, and I was very sad. I sat, I waited, I tried not to move too much or overreact, but the damage was done. Saturday, I tried to rest for most of the day, but in the evening I bent over to dust something, because I am insane, and *"Pop!"* again. Pop goes the back.

I'm in pretty bad pain – walking hurts, but not as bad as sitting. Laying down is agony. So I've been walking around, hoping to ease it up a bit. When I walk I look  like – Gerry! We're a matched set, now. All we need are his and hers walkers.

I'm flying out next Saturday for Texas, and although I'm certain my back will be fine by then I'm not looking forward to the flight. Or to the lugging around of the suitcases that makes up most of my trips.

I just have to convince myself NOT to do any lifting, heavy or otherwise. Today we had a family meeting where I explained to the kids that the lax attitude they'd adopted about doing their chores and helping out had to change. Two months out of the routine will make anyone a little lazy, especially a nine- and eleven-year-old!

So they've agreed not to make faces when I ask them to do their chores. Even better they'll try not to put me in a position where I *have* to ask. *We're still pre-teen here, and I'm going to enjoy every minute of it while I can.*

This afternoon Gerry and the kids put away all of the food stuffs so our dining room is looking much more like a *dining* room! There are still details to be ironed out, but it's pretty much finished.

I'm absolutely in LOVE with the new bathroom. Having it on the ground floor has had a positive impact on our family, and it's the best decision we could have made as we work toward Gerry's recovery. Ground floor laundry is also wonderful in that it lets Gerry do a load every now and then, especially nice when I'm away.

The kitchen itself is a dream. It's lovely, a wonderful complement to the dining room and the rest of the house. It's quite modern, but has a *"period"* feel. I love the chair/picture rail in the kitchen that matches the dining room. It looks so wonderful – so organic – as if it were the way the house was built originally.

Our young, creative contractor was a dream to work with and we're very happy. We saved money in lots of ways by buying *"scratch and dent"* appliances, looking for bargains on bathroom tiles, putting together our own lighting fixtures instead of buying pre-made, etc. Our line of credit came through, so it's now a happy and snug part of our mortgage!

The best part? The financial damage was less than we budgeted, *how often can one say that?*

October Eighth
Gerry's Status
St. Paul, MN

When I was a little girl one of my favorite books was
<u>Little House In The Big Woods</u> – the predecessor to the
<u>Little House On The Prairie</u> series.

Here we are, living in Laura Ingalls Wilder country, and
our Minnesota story thus far feels like a chapter out of
Little House. The winter ice storm we drove through to
get here, Gerry's horrific back pain, the death of our
sweet old cat, Mr. Butkis; it seemed things were going so
far wrong.

Gerry and I talked about it at the time – he, lying in bed
because he was in so much pain from his *"mystery illness;"*
me, sweaty and exhausted from the unpacking, putting
away, building of shelves and wardrobes.

I remember that day as if it were yesterday. I had such
guilt for dragging the family across the country, only to
have all of this horrible stuff rain down on us.

Gerry was philosophical – *"It's like we're pioneers, as if
we're fighting through our first year on the prairie."*

Pioneers, just a few short blocks from the local Caribou
Coffee.

Since February, life's been a blur; doctors, tests, more
doctors, more tests, and then the diagnosis; *Multiple
Myeloma.*

Since our move there has been so much garbage – so
much crap – hardest on Gerry, but not a picnic for the
kids and me.

But – honestly – not really so *bad*, after all.

Life isn't supposed to be happy and fun all the time. Sometimes in the hardest situations there's a type of thankfulness we can feel for just getting through. A gratitude which is so sweet and embracing, it aches. There's that giddiness in doing something like this together, as a family, and surviving.

When I consider all of the stuff we've been through since February, it feels as if we're working our way through a dark forest. Sometimes the trees are very close together, sometimes the ground is swampy and our steps are uncertain.

But sometimes it's quite nice, with views of the sky above, or the stars at night.

And now we've walked into a clearing – a meadow – where we'll be while Gerry gets healthier and healthier. The transplant went beautifully – as well as anyone could expect – and the doctors at Mayo were very impressed with Gerry's resilience. My husband, the overachiever!

Finally Gerry was home, we were *all* home; the kids, Gerry, me, Gerry's mom Elaine, Atticus, Gigi – we were a family again. So much happened while we were apart, and now we're together and trying to figure out how we fit together again.

The kids have grown, I've grown. We have a new kitchen, a new kitten, and a new Gerry.

The nurse kept telling Gerry during his actual transplant on September 1, *"Today is your birthday – Happy Birthday!"*

"Great," I thought, *"Just what we need, another Virgo in the house..."*

Gerry's so new that he'll have to have all of his childhood immunizations again in about a year. He's like a baby, bald and adorable, *and I feel as terrified as I did when Hannah came home.*

A new friend wrote to me on the day of Gerry's transplant, which happened to be her Day Plus 100 after her own stem cell transplant for Multiple Myeloma. She's kindly been updating us, walking ahead of us in the woods, marking the path.

As a family we feel – *scared.* But glad to be together. We have no idea how long we'll be able to stay in this "meadow" before we have to go back into the woods. How big IS this meadow? Is it a prairie?

Can we build a house here, write a series of books and make them into a TV series starring a self-reverential actor?

We have our moments when it becomes too much *(usually I'm the one having those moments)*, and then we pull together as a family and find some sense in the whole mess.

If we can't make sense, at least we try to make a joke.

OCTOBER FIFTEENTH
AUSTIN IS AUSOME
AUSTIN, TX

A kid rode by on a bike yesterday morning with a tie dyed T shirt which read, *"Keep Austin Weird."* Love it!

I have this overwhelming sense that something is on the horizon, but I have no idea what it is. Gerry is recovering, not at the miracle speed that we experienced immediately after the stem cell transplant, but every day he's a bit better.

It doesn't help that I'm away so much; that's hard. So here I am in Austin, paying the mortgage and fretting. Laying awake, listening to 14th-century love songs.

I have a tendency to chat too much when I'm around folks, a side effect of teaching and lecturing for a living. My chatter recently has such a brittle, one-sided vein to it that is hard for even ME to listen, so I can only imagine how difficult it is for someone else to absorb.

I need to curtail it a bit for my own sanity, and perhaps be a bit shallower when I interact with so many folks? Every day is another experiment in working things through.

I'm glad I'm here, but I've yet to really settle in and feel *comfortable* in my skin in Texas. Tomorrow on the way into the shop I'll find a place where I can get a nice bowl of oatmeal for breakfast. *It's hard to have a bad day when you start with a hot, fiber-filled breakfast!*

OCTOBER NINETEENTH
DIDN'T EVEN SEE IT COMING...
AUSTIN, TX

The folks in my classes in Austin have been among the best I've taught! Engaged, funny, lively and *very* quick with the knitting.

They pick up concepts as fast as I can throw them down, and their passion for knitting – and for life – is so strong it has a taste.

As I said to my class last night, *"If you could arrange for the average temperature to drop 40 degrees, I'd move to Austin in a heartbeat!"* Oh, wait – that would make this St. Paul...

Having said that, this has been an incredibly draining trip. My current mental state, along with this feeling that I just can't rest, leave me feeling fragile. The heat isn't helping – I don't do well with heat.

See what a delicate plant I am? My resources – mental, emotional and stamina – were tapped so far that I was running on fumes. But as I left the class last night the air seemed lighter and cooler, not so thick and hot, and I felt like a new woman. Amazing how a breeze will lift my spirits.

Teaching – as with falling in love, discovering an author, or finding a favorite TV show – is *chemistry*. My own unique blend of instruction may not work well for every student, and once or twice a year someone just doesn't *"get"* me or my style of teaching.

I had a student yesterday who was *not* enjoying the fine subtleties and delicate bouquet that is my teaching style. She left early in the class, and it affected me more strongly than it should have.

I can't change the basics of who I am. I try to be as authentic as I can when I teach, for better or for worse. Usually it works pretty well, but this was an instance of failure.

The rest of the class was amazing. They circled around me, and I felt entirely surrounded by human Conestoga wagons. Eventually I calmed down. It took me longer than I'd expected, and I felt quite silly and terribly emotional. *Boo and Hoo.*

My own personal situation is rough now, and although I shouldn't let it invade my teaching, it's hard to keep everything compartmentalized. In all honesty that's kind of against my personal philosophy.

You'll never find a balance in life if you don't put everything on the scale...

October Twenty–Second

Max's Sock

St. Paul, MN

Max and I took Shiloh to the vet today for his final kitten booster shots and his worming medicine. He's a full pound heavier than he was three weeks ago, and he's adorable.

While sitting in the waiting room I pulled out a sock I'm working on and showed it to Max. He said he liked it, and his eyes lit up when I told him it was for *him*. A very nice moment. *He's excited to see how I put the heel in his sock later.*

The stress of Gerry's illness coupled with my traveling is definitely taking its toll on the kids. Max tends to hold in more than Hannah. It gives the illusion that he's so very easy going – and he is – but he can only take so much before it all becomes too much. So I'm making him a sock, two in fact, and giving myself something to work on during flights.

There's a transit ad here in the Twin Cities where a man grows old while sitting in his car. Gerry's still at the *"missing hair stage"* of his cancer recovery, and thus looks older than he will in a few weeks.

It seems as though this ad captures Gerry's experience of the past few months. Perhaps I notice Gerry's changes more than the kids do because I travel? I'm hoping by the New Year we'll feel as though we're watching that transit ad in reverse.

Today Oprah was about cancer. I couldn't help but notice that the two folks they interviewed were both *very* healthy-looking. There were no great changes physically in their appearance, no major diminishment in their mobility.

Randy Pausch, author of <u>The Last Lecture</u> and victim of pancreatic cancer, was doing pushups. How surreal that must seem, to be so ill, but look so healthy. That's definitely not the situation for Gerry.

Tomorrow we go to Gerry's oncologist for the first time since our return from Mayo. Tests will be run, but I'll be watching the doctor and nurses to see how they react to Gerry after not having seen him for almost three months. That's my own personal test.

October Twenty-Fourth
Doctor, Doctor!
St. Paul, MN

Gerry's doctor visit yesterday was pretty uneventful. The doctor was very happy with Gerry's lab work and said we don't need to see him again until after Thanksgiving.

Gerry's so weak, though, that they may put him back on Zometa to increase his strength. Gerry told the doctor he'd just like to be able to *"toss around a ball with his son,"* which made me lower my head over my knitting so neither could see I was crying.

Thankfully, right around the corner from our home are triplet boys with a Super-Dad who is a baseball *and* football coach (and an ER Doc). Max loves hanging out with these kids, they have a huge yard and there's always some kind of pick-up game going on.

So, if Max doesn't have Gerry to toss a football with him right now, he has the next best thing – good friends nearby with a cool dad. Very good for Max, he needs that.

Gerry needs a haircut. He's clinging to his last few strands of hair and is in definite danger of entering Smeagol territory. I'm pushing him to get one because today knitting blogger and author Crazy Aunt Purl – aka, Laurie Perry – arrives in Minnesota! I'm SO excited to see her, and she reminded me on the phone yesterday that twice before we've gotten together on October

197

25th (which is a monumental day for her), so here we are again – getting together on our day.

When I edited the book of essays <u>Cheaper Than Therapy</u>, I asked Laurie if she'd contribute something. Then I beat her over the head via email until I got it. Nice, huh?

Her essay, *"Drunk, Divorced & Covered in Cat Hair"* was exceptionally funny, and eventually she added to it, making it a self-help book which has sold, oh, 583 times as well as the original <u>Cheaper Than Therapy</u>. And it deserves to – it's great!

In the book she writes about a class she took with me at Unwind Yarn Shop in Burbank, CA. When I read the chapter where I'm mentioned for the first time I was preparing for a class in Petaluma, CA. I almost burst into tears. She's very kind.

But then again, I burst into tears reading a coffee can these days. With any luck I'll see her tonight. I'd like to kidnap her and drag her over to meet the family.

Who am I kidding? I want her to see the new kitchen and kitten!

Miracle-Hope

The hardest thing about this whole adventure (for me, at least) are the folks I've started calling *Hyper-Hopers.*

They're folks who say, *"Gerry will beat this, the doctors aren't always right! Don't lose hope!"* They desperately need for me to jump on the Hope Train with them. When I run into someone like this, I feel that I *must* hope for the same things they're hoping for, or I'm letting them down.

And it's not just plain, simple hope they want me to espouse *(we have that in bucketfuls)*, but it's an irrational XTREME hope they need me to embrace.

I've come to the conclusion that because *they* may not entirely believe what they're saying, it's vital to them that *I* believe what they're saying – almost as if my sanction of their belief is what's most important.

It's like asking me to help them out by carrying their purse, or books, or belief structure. They ask too much of folks who are just trying to get through a very rough patch in life.

The folks who insist that *"Gerry will beat this!"* – how do they *know?*

They want to use Gerry's illness as some kind of morality play. A truly positive person will recover, while a less positive person will fade. Trial by cancer.

But I think – at the heart of it – they want us to do what they do every day; *ignore mortality.* Like so many folks, we used to be able to do this. We can't do it anymore. And it's not a bad thing, this understanding that life will have an end.

199

Some have told me that *"God will work a miracle, Gerry will be cured!"* but that's too easy to say, and ignores the responsibility we each bear for our own lives. There have been miracles. Our kids are miracles. That Gerry and I even *found* each other is miraculous.

And the fact that we can laugh through this truly terrifying experience is *also* a miracle.

But I do not – not for one minute – believe that we'll go to the oncologist tomorrow and he'll say, *"You're totally clean, no cancer, all signs are perfect and you'll live to a ripe old age..."*

Of course, that's the catch-22. If I say out loud that I don't believe there will be a *"Hallelujah! Cancer is Cured!"* bona-fide miracle, it's a Gotcha! moment. *"See, that's why there hasn't been a miracle! You didn't believe!"*

Oh, goody, more crap for me to carry around!

These *Hyper-Hopers*, however, are the minority. They are so different from the many kind folks who simply say, *"We'll be thinking of you"* or *"We'll be praying for you"* – which is lovely.

They don't need anything back from us. They don't need us to say, *"Yes, you're right, we WILL beat this!"* or anything like that. They don't even need me to say, *"Thank you,"* although I do, because they're offering this as a gift.

When I want to convey a sense of solidarity with sick friends, I've now learned to say, *"We'll be thinking of you..."* Sometimes introducing the prayer thing can be a burden to the person who's ill, but if folks want to pray for us, then that's fine.

Just don't expect to pray with us. That's too personal.

So here are two truisms we've learned in this stage of the journey:

1. Unrealistic Hope is expensive, and we're on a budget.

2. When someone is in a very bad situation, don't tell them what <u>you want them</u> to hope for (i.e., recovery). Just hope they have a good day. That's enough.

And, so far? Most of our doctors have been right – and they've been a kind of miracle workers, too. The fact is, disease happens. Sometimes it shortens life. It sucks and it's unfair, but it doesn't have to ruin – or even diminish – a life.

We don't spend every day shopping for caskets, but we also have a realistic outlook on where our family will be in three, five, or seven years. No one can tell the future, but we can prepare. I know what it's like to not prepare. I experienced that when I saw my mother work like a dog for ten years to crawl out of the financial hole my dad's death had put us in. *Not on my watch.*

OCTOBER TWENTY-
SIXTH

FALLING FOR

CAP

ST. PAUL, MN

It's Fall – Autumn in Minnesota – which is exceptionally

beautiful! And the best part, I got to share a bit of our lovely St. Paul crispness with Laurie! I picked her up and brought her home on Wednesday for dinner. She met Gerry and the kids, Atticus and the cats. *(Atticus and*

Hannah are both in love with her, and the kitten absolutely adored her. Gigi was noncommittal, she's that way.)

It was a wonderful evening, and Gerry proclaimed Laurie *"Delightful!"* And thus, a few new CAP (Crazy Aunt Purl) fans were created! *Arf!* In fact, Gerry was SO taken with her that insisted on going to Barnes & Noble on Thursday night with the kids for Laurie's book signing. It worked out beautifully. Laurie was funny, self-effacing, dear and charming, what a treat!

I think everyone in the crowd was ready to take her home, and I swear several women were cell phoning single sons and nephews to get their butts over to the B&N to meet this amazing, sexy, blonde best-selling author!

Later Laurie, Jennie The Potter and I went out and had rich, fatty foods and many, many beers. Well deserved wind-down time for all, especially the hard-working Laurie! *I think if we could have kept her here for another few days we'd have another Minnesota convert.*

I'm enjoying having Max's socks as my on-flight traveling knitting. It makes me feel connected to the family in a physical way when I'm on the road. As I was knitting his sock during Laurie's talk he kept glancing over at me with a big smile on his face. He likes his socks.

I flew into Denver today and was picked up at the airport. I hadn't had lunch, and felt oddly light headed. Airsick, almost, which usually doesn't happen to me. I chalked it up to having a beer *(or three)* last night, not my normal routine before I travel.

But then my host reminded me of the change in altitude. Aha! I'm DEFINITELY feeling the effects. *Crazy, man.*

October Twenty-Ninth
Altitude Hang Over
Denver, CO

Wow, I feel like I've been on a three-day bender! I had no idea that I'd be so affected by the altitude, but for a few days I did not feel much like myself. Not that I'm not often light-headed and giddy, but I'm usually not *so* light-headed and giddy (and tired, and dehydrated, and short of breath...).

The classes were at a historical education center in Littleton, with horses and geese, folks in period costume and lots of hay. A group of costumed *"pioneer kids"* went speeding by on a little motorized cart like some wacky , surreal Amish roller coaster.

Along with one of the oddest physical sensations of my life *(being 5,000 feet above my usual level of existence)*, I had one of the best physical sensations of my life – The Massage. Not long after I got back to my most enjoyable room, a good friend came by with her massage table and all the stuff that massage therapists usually carry around. She'd emailed me a few weeks before my visit, offering a full body massage to help offset the recent back pain that I'd been suffering.

Stress has been the word for the past few months, and finding ways to deal with it – humor, family time, knitting, walks – has been a constant struggle. I hadn't realized how all this stress had manifested itself physically inside of my body until it finally escaped.

Although I don't have anyone to judge her against, my massage friend was exceptionally skilled. After being worked on for an hour I felt like a new person.

I haven't been writing, designing or creating as much as I have in past years. Projects that I'd hoped to have finished are piling up like haystacks in my brain. In my lowest moments I fear I won't be able to get back to the place I was at a year ago.

At that time I was looking ahead toward new book ideas, design ideas, and feeling relatively secure in my place as a teacher and writer. I'm not feeling so secure now.

I'm trying to roll with it, not let it freak me out or stymie me more than necessary. That seems like the best way to work through this period without making it worse by panicking in slow motion. As I sit down to sketch, do some research or write a bit, so many things come to the top of my mind. Go here, do this, get that done. Be a mom, be a provider, be a healer and organize future teaching engagements.

The emotional and physical energy involved in meeting dozens of folks is more draining than one might think. It's true that I get so much out of my teaching. Now I'm receiving all this love, care and good vibes, but I'm not able to pour them into my designs as I had been before.

I'm losing energy. My kids will tell you that as I lose energy, I tend to get short-tempered. Perhaps writing about it will help me barrel through? Or maybe I'm looking for a path around the boulder I seem to be facing? I have about nine days before I leave for Virginia, longer at home than I've had for a while.

I'm not going to push anything. I'm going to see if I can just let some new stuff – new designs, new books, maybe a DVD – flow naturally. Fretting is a damn. But not fretting is a bitch. I need another massage.

I'm afraid I grossed out my class with a recipe for dip - equal parts peanut butter, ketchup and red onion - that I love to eat with Fritos. *Must be a low altitude thing.*

November

November Fifth
The Rules
St. Paul, MN

Anyone who's taken a class with me knows my rules. Yes, free spirit Annie has rules. *Obey or suffer.* So for those of you who haven't yet taken a class with me, here they are:

Rule #1

You are NOT allowed to say anything about yourself in class that you wouldn't want to hear your daughter say about herself.

This seems pretty much self-explanatory *(except for that time I had Joan Crawford in a class)*. I don't like folks to talk themselves down – they pay me good money to do that myself, and if I let them do it, then I'm superfluous. Seriously, though, words have power.

Not using certain words – i.e., *"I stink!" "I suck!" "I can't do this, I'm stupid!"* is one way to get my students to begin to wrap their minds around the concept that they have *all* the knowledge they need already within them. My job is to bring this knowledge out so they can connect the dots and remember the techniques.

Rule #2

When I'm talking, I should be the *only* one talking.

This is from my Brownie Leader days, but it serves me in good stead. Talking is a distraction and disrespectful, not just to me, but to the other students. I lose my place, I become distracted, and then we lose precious time while I vamp about my 5th grade sleep-away camp experience, frantically trying to remember where I was in the class.

Plus, the folks sitting next to the talker have a hard time fully concentrating. *I do this for the student's own safety, that annoyed knitter next to someone talking nonstop has sharp objects within reach.*

RULE #3

Do NOT rip out in my class!

I don't mean that folks should never rip out – I rip out frequently. My intention is that if folks make a mistake that they can't solve in class, I'd like them to let me know, and we can go over it together and use it as a learning experience. I *like* folks to make mistakes. *I often say that if one isn't making a mistake in my classes, one isn't trying.*

Mistakes – if we choose to embrace them and learn from them – can be a way to discover several new ways to do something. But I have to be able to see the mistake myself in order to give any sensible suggestion on how something might be fixed.

What usually happens is that as soon as I pick up a swatch and look at it, the knitter has a mental connection and they'll understand very clearly what happened, even before I do!

Sometimes it just takes someone else looking at your work for something to click.

NOVEMBER THIRTEENTH
SILLY, BUT HUMAN
ST. PAUL, MN

After returning from my last teaching engagement I had another chance to see my family doing well in my absence. It's hard for all of them when I'm gone, hard for me, too. But it's lovely to see them functioning so well. They're getting to know the Twin Cities better than

I do – visiting museums and historic sites when I'm away – and I'm a little jealous.

Being away from Gerry for a few days at a time allows me to see changes in him that might not be as apparent to the kids. We don't really have any other regular visitors in our lives, a few friends who come by every two weeks or so, but nothing like when we lived in NJ and had the same folks dropping by every few days.

So I'm *it* as far as any other adults seeing Gerry's recovery. And I can tell that it's wearing on Gerry. He's lonely for some companionship besides me, the kids and the pets.

Both of us are concerned that his back isn't better. He has a great deal of pain. We feel that we're in a waiting game, waiting to see what the Mayo clinic says on his Day Plus 100 visit, waiting for a call back from his

oncologist so he can get a referral for a back specialist or physical therapy

Waiting for him to get better.

He is better – we think. Physically he's not as well as he was just before the transplant, which is a disappointment to both of us. But the transplant and chemo were really rough, and it's hard to recover from them.

Hannah calls him, *"Little Dad"* – lovingly – and he accepts it, also with love. I'm ashamed of how much his reduced height seems to matter to me; in the scheme of life it's so unimportant. I need to keep remembering that. It could be ugly and hard to take without the love..

Travel is rough. I have always hated flying, for me it's barely tolerable at best. I'm taller than the average woman, and I have long, long legs that bang up against the seat in front of me.

I hate being on someone else's schedule, hate being told to put my liquid concealer in a baggie *(because evidently the terrorists hate our flawless complexions)*, and I hate walking for what feels like miles to go from gate to gate. Over carpet. Dragging luggage.

This week my trip to Virginia entailed a total of four flights on small commuter airlines, the kind with jets that can't pull up to a gate, so one must walk out on the tarmac, up the stairs and onto the plane. Each time I got to the top of the stairs I'd pause, turn, and thrust both arms up into the air, waving the peace sign with both hands, *a la* Nixon.

No one thought it was funny *(except one woman who laughed in Cincinnati)*. Each time I deplaned I waved like one of the Beatles. *Once again, not funny. Eh.* All those steps, all that cramming my legs into small spaces led to a visit to the doc today because my knee *"went out"* during the night while I was asleep. Rest, she says, is the thing.

However, I do love *knitting* while I travel. Knitting Max's Socks and picturing his face when I show him my progress has been a lot of fun. He loves them, loves the color, the yarn, the fact they're for him! They fit – but *just* – so I am going to take off the toes and knit them out longer.

One of my dreams is to take Gerry and the kids to Scotland at some point in the next few years,-hopefully as part of a teaching trip. It feels to me that it would be an important thing for us to do as a family.

I wonder how long it would take to travel by boat? At least I'd get a lot of knitting done!

NOVEMBER TWENTY-
FIRST
EDMONTON
REFLECTIONS
EDMONTON, ALBERTA
CANADA

When I think about what kind of person I am, which we all do sometimes, I feel that I'm someone folks don't consider dispassionately. The more tired I am, the more exhausted or worn out, the less I'm able to control the sharper points of my being. *Which is not necessarily a bad thing, but it feels better to have it under control.*

I arrived in Edmonton after a wonderful but tiring weekend of teaching 45 women in Banff, and a long car and bus ride. After settling into my hotel I turned my

210

mind to two more days of teaching. But keeping that amount of students functioning, tapping into their consciousness with my own tools of humor, knitting skill and a small amount of pushing is exhausting. But satisfying.

I received a very kind email from a student in one of my

classes on Tuesday, a student who will probably not know just how much her kindness meant to me today.

Another great kindness was the ride to the airport by a friend who has the distinction of having been married to a Royal Canadian Mounted Police Officer – a Mountie – while living in the Yukon. *Be still my heart.*

That is something that very few women can say, but I suspect many would like to...

NOVEMBER TWENTY-SECOND
GRATITUDE OF HOME
AN EXPLANATION IN SEVERAL PARTS
ST. PAUL, MN

Home. I love home so much.

When I was twelve years old my dad lost his business. He'd started a company to create the first single place hovercraft in the US, and had signed a personal note which, when called in, pretty much wiped us out. My dad was a genius, but not terribly savvy. *And sometimes kind of a jerk.*

Our parents didn't share all of this financial difficulty with my brother and me, they just sucked it up (and fought a lot). We had a very, very tense household. The financial tension was manifest in so many ways; frustration, alcohol abuse and – worst of all – violence. Everything came to a head when I was in the seventh grade.

One day not long after Thanksgiving, I walked home from school and found a notice on our door that our home would be sold in a sheriff's auction in 30 days. I guess my parents were in denial, or thought they would be the first to get the news. I'm certain they didn't envision me finding out this way. So we started moving from rented house to rented house. Then, after my father died, from apartment to apartment.

During high school I used to drive my aqua '65 AMC Rambler through an area of Toledo called Ottawa Hills, and dream about having a *real* home someday. I've heard that Virgos can be very home-centered, and that's certainly true of me. When I went off to college, my mother and brother moved into a two bedroom apartment. *Why spend all that money for an extra bedroom that will only be used a few weeks a year?*

I realized that any home I'd have from then on would be of my own making. So I made lots of homes.

Wherever I lived, I'd strive to make it a nice space, as well thought out and beautifully furnished as I could afford. This may have been part of why I became interested in set design. I like creating good ground plans with nice flow, with a space for everyone, creating comforting, restful areas to relax. *I love home.*

I discovered knitting when I was 25. And, more than religion, art, music, nature – more than anything that had so far defined me as a person – knitting felt like *home* to me. In knitting I could find the same comfort, I could ease myself into the same frame of mind, as I'd find in my home on a cozy winter night. All this simply by pulling out some yarn and needles and knitting deep into my soul.

When I began knitting and designing for a living back in the early 80s, I think I became enmeshed in what I can only describe as *Queen Midas Syndrome.* For better or for worse, I turned what I loved best into gold.

Unfortunately, I lacked the maturity to make this devil's bargain. I let myself be taken advantage of by the very devil that seduced me, and eventually I found that I was destroying the thing which brought me the most joy.

For this, and for a few other reasons, I put away knitting for many years. During that time I began to more clearly define myself – my hopes, dreams, goals – and I found my heart, my Gerry.

Gerry and I wandered into each other's lives in an unusual way, almost pre-destined, and I can't help but feel that both of our maternal grandmothers *(who oddly resemble each other in family photographs, go figure...)* somehow got together in the great beyond and gave us a little shove in each other's direction. A hillbilly *shidduch*..

NOVEMBER TWENTY-THIRD
GRATITUDE OF LOVE
A CONTINUATION
ST. PAUL, MN

So I spent most of my life not dating very heavily. I'm well, an unusual looking woman. Beautiful in many ways, but not in the more *conventional* ways.

And, sadly, a lot of guys are shallow when assessing potential date material. So I figured I was destined to be a Methodist Nun. I would call my mom, moaning that I wasn't married with no prospects on the horizon. Her astringent response?

"Honey, if you really wanted to be married, you'd be married."

Which was true. I've known lots of folks who have married because it was the *thing to do*, because they felt like they *should* be married, or because it was one of their life goals. If the goal was simply to be married, my mom's comment implied, then I was strong and directed enough to do what needed to be done to get married.

But that wasn't the goal, and the goal I'd set for myself couldn't be rushed. My goal wasn't to be married – it was to be in love, and to be loved. And here's the tricky part – without turning myself inside out. *Which, ironically, is an easier goal to contemplate when you don't have folks busting down your door and asking for your hand.*

So I lived my life as a single woman, moving around a bit but, for the most part, thinking of myself as a New Yorker.

New York City is an exceptional place to be single – better than anywhere else I've lived in that regard. There are families, yes, but there are also many transitional single folks. In NYC it's easier to think of singleness as a valid, long-term alternative to marriage. Or maybe it's just that many folks who move to NYC tend to place marriage low on their list of goals?

So I kicked around New York, working in corporate jobs and then knitting for a living. I went to grad school for theatrical set and costume design and returned to New York, living in Brooklyn, and working as an assistant on Broadway and as a stylist for TV and photo shoots.

One of the plays I worked on was a stage production of the movie, *My Favorite Year*. After opening night my services as a costume assistant and shoe-buyer were no longer required, so I found myself at home in my Brooklyn kitchen one Autumn Saturday morning.

I had been a fan of the Wisconsin Public Radio quiz show, *What Do You Know*, and I listened on WNYC whenever I was free on Saturday mornings. On this particular morning I called in and – lo and behold – actually got through and was in the queue to answer the qualifying question; *"What was the first couple to share the presidential bedroom?"* When my turn came I decided honesty was the best policy.

> *– I don't know the answer, but I really, really want to be on the show...*
> *– You could say, "The Fords."*
> *– "The Fords?"*
> *– You're RIGHT!*

And thus it came to pass that I became a contestant. In the game a contestant is paired with someone from the studio audience, and together they're asked three questions. If they get these three questions right, they can choose to answer two more for a grand prize and risk losing everything if they answer incorrectly. I was paired with Tom, a nice man in the Madison, Wisconsin studio audience. Together Tom and I set out to win it all.

I pretty much talked non-stop for 45 minutes. Or at least it felt like that. I remember trying to be considerate, and let Tom speak, but I was far too nervous and excited. With each question Tom and I took full advantage of the host's *schtick* of giving the correct answer when asked in the right way. Before long, we'd reached the pinnacle of the five questions, and we were Big Kielbasa winners. The end.

Or so I thought.

Two weeks after the show I received a letter with a Madison, WI postmark, but a Queens, NY return address. It was a sweet, charming and funny note from a guy who'd heard me on the radio, and thought that I, too, sounded sweet, funny and charming.

He wrote that he was living in Queens, and that he had *no* idea where I lived or what my last name was. He only knew that I lived in Brooklyn, because I said so on the air. He explained that I was receiving this letter because he had called the producer of the radio show and she had agreed to forward it on to me.

But what was I supposed to do with it? I asked my married friends, and they all said, *"Stay away from this person!"* My single friends told me that if I didn't call him, they would.

At the time I was costuming a production of the Yiddish theater classic, *The Dybbuk*, at a girl's Yeshiva and asked the all-female cast what they thought. *"Call him, call him!"* they all said. One asked, *"Is he Jewish?"*

I didn't call him, I sent a Christmas card. So he called me. And we agreed on the phone to meet a few days before Christmas for coffee.

> *A: How will I know you?*
> *G: I'm 5'8" and I have a beard...*
> *A: Oh. [pause] I'm 5'11" and I have red hair...*

We agreed to meet at the famous-and-now-gone Peacock Cafe in Greenwich Village *(where they switched the coffee for the Folder's Crystals in the TV ad from the 1970s)*. I arrived early so I could settle in near the back of the restaurant and have a bowl of soup, keeping an eye on the front door.

It seemed that every man in New York who was 5'8" with a beard came to the Peacock Cafe that night. Old, young, handsome, surly, pompous – they were *all* there. A convention of 5'8" bearded men.

I was nervous and anxious. None of these guys looked very friendly. Then I noticed that sitting near the front of the restaurant was a guy in an ill-fitting sport coat who looked as nervous as I felt. So I walked over to his table.

> *A: Are you Gerry?*
> *G: Yes.*
> *A: I'm Annie. I have a table near the back*
> *   that's a little nicer. Do you want to join me?*

So we met. Both of us had stretched the truth. I was more like 6', he was closer to 5'7"

We had coffee, then went for a long walk and ended by having a beer at the Prince Street Bar. That was date number one. By March he'd moved in, and by Mother's Day we were engaged. We were married in August.

When I called my mother to tell her we were engaged, she was *almost* okay with us living together *("As long as you are getting married, Annette.")*, and was not as troubled as I feared by the fact that we'd have an interfaith marriage *("You wouldn't be the first...")*. But she was very troubled by the height difference. *"Oh, Annette. Are you sure you love him?"*

As we were preparing to walk down the aisle, hand in hand, at the Old Music Building at Rutgers where we were married, Gerry told me that August 21, 1993 was exactly nine months since he'd heard me on the radio, November 21, 1992. August 21, 2007 was our 14th anniversary.

NOVEMBER TWENTY-FIFTH
GRATITUDE OF DIFFERENCES
MORE THAN ONE RIGHT WAY
ST. PAUL, MN

I met Gerry during the period in my life when I wasn't doing much knitting. *Okay, I wasn't doing any knitting.* As a matter of fact, for about ten years I didn't knit at all.

And, having put aside something I loved so much, I appreciated it in a much deeper way after my hiatus. The prodigal knitter.

I had come crashing out of the gate with knitting in the early 1980s. From the moment I picked up the needles I knew that yarn and needles were going to be a huge part of my destiny. That sounds insane, but knitters know what I mean.

Knitting and knit design became the main activity in my life. Every waking moment was spent knitting, sketching or swatching. When I see new knitters and designers who are going through their *obsession period* of knitting, I entirely understand. In many ways I'm still in it, but I prefer to think of it as my passion rather than obsession.

But I knit *weird*. Back in 1983 a good friend, Ellyn, taught me how to make a knit stitch – and I moved to Texas the next day. I figured out the purl stitch on my own, but apparently I figured it out wrong. I was trying to imitate, in reverse, what was happening when I worked my knit stitch, and thus stumbled onto the Eastern purl *(aka, "Lazy purl")* and adopted it as my own.

Without realizing it, I was a Combination knitter, which was a lot harder to be in the early 80s than it is today.

I hear folks bemoan the state of the world – and I agree there is a lot that's not pretty – but we're at an astounding point in history where there is mobility between classes and cultures that we haven't witnessed before.

Here is one, perhaps frivolous, example: In the past, generally younger women and servants sported skirts that were shorter than those worn by higher class women. At certain times there were strict societal and even legal restrictions on skirt lengths.

But now – as at no other time in history – it is possible for *any* woman, from *any* class, to wear *any* length skirt and still be accepted, even *fashionable*.

In my eyes this is a victory of individuality over a monolithic authority, and gives me hope for every aspect of society.

In the first half of the 20th century alone we've run the gamut from micro-mini to floor-length skirt, but each in its own sanctioned fashion parameters. We live in a time right now when a mini-skirt and a long skirt can walk down the street together and both be considered fashionable.

In the same way, different methods of knitting are more generally accepted now than they were several years ago. I can't speak for 100 or 300 years ago, but from research I've done it seems that sometime in the 1920s there became a *"correct"* way to knit, accepted as standard in the Western world. And that standard way was what can be defined as Western knitting.

It's a short hop from creating a standard knitting method to calling every other method "wrong," and I, like many other closet Combination knitters, was caught up in that sense of shame that my knitting didn't quite measure up. The fabric was lovely, the tension was even, I was a very fast knitter, but folks felt compelled to stop when I knit in public to tell me how *wrong* my method was.

Whenever I'd knit out in the open, the exchange would go something like this:

> *– I just had to tell you I've never seen anyone knit so fast!*
> *– Thank you.*
> *– And your stitches are so even!*
> *– Thank you.*
> *– But I couldn't help but notice that you're knitting <u>wrong</u>.*

This began to weigh heavily on my soul. Sometimes I couldn't keep the anger internal, which was bad news for me, and worse for the poor person who was trying to correct me. I was too stubborn to stop knitting in a way that felt comfortable, but I became too agitated to enjoy my knitting when folks continuously told me it was *wrong*.

Things came to a head after a trip to Europe when a woman in Germany took my knitting out of my hands to show me the right way to knit. In direct response to that incident, I found myself being rude to a woman who was doing nothing worse than staring at my knitting in an airport in Brussels. *"This has to stop,"* I thought on the plane back to the states. *"It's just tearing me up. And it isn't doing much for those around me..."*

So I put my knitting aside and went to grad school to study theatrical design. With the exception of the odd theatrical knit piece, I didn't knit for quite a while, only picking up my needles recreationally when I became pregnant with my son ten years later.

Although giving up knitting was hard, think how much more difficult it must be to consider giving up one's concept of the Eternal, sexual preference or cultural identity. Yet society has asked just that of many folks, sometimes with dire consequences for those who refused to conform.

I don't want to compare a voluntary, recreational activity like knitting to a more serious subject, but I believe we can use our passions *[in my case, knitting]* to bridge understanding to people and events that may not be within our own life experience. This is one way that imagination informs empathy.

We have certain taboos in society, but it's good to see folks rethinking them instead of just accepting views which have been handed down. This is how a society evolves. At one time, it was odd to see a tall woman/ short man couple. It's still a hard visual for some folks to get past *(my own mother was more troubled by my height difference with Gerry than she was with our religious differences)*

221

but there are a *lot* more *Betty & Barney* couples out there these days. *Go team Rubble!*

I was fortunate that my return to knitting coincided with the printing of an article by Priscilla Gibson Roberts in *Interweave Knits* magazine outlining the various methods of knitting. And there was my knitting style, in black and white, sanctioned by a real knitting authority. Combination Knitting, named and legitimate. *Hallelujah.*

It's hard to express the calmness and sense of direction that legitimacy imparts. Being a maverick can be exciting, but it's wearying. Knowing you have a connection with others who do something you love so dearly in the *same* way is an indescribable joy.

Along with designing and writing, I teach Combination knitting now, not to *convert* anyone to my way of knitting, but rather to help my students understand the architecture and grammar of their own knitting, however they knit.

Much in the way that by taking French classes I began to better understand principles of English grammar, learning a new way to form a knit or purl stitch can help any knitter better comprehend how to diagnose and improve their knitted fabric.

I was so lucky to read that article, so fortunate to find my place as a Combination knitter. I've discovered hundreds of other Combination knitters who have come out of the yarn closet, bravely knitting in public and explaining with patience and passion how different types of knitting are just different ways of looking at loops.

But my French still leaves a lot to be desired. *Sacre Bleu!*

DECEMBER

December First
Settling In
St. Paul, MN

It's a snowy Minnesota weekend, long in coming. A weekend that's good for cups of hot tea or chocolate, sledding and knitting. I'll take the latter, thank you very much...

According to the records and the locals, November is usually a much snowier month. There's a lot of catch-up to do in order to get the snowfall/rainfall levels back up to a decent place. No one likes a drought.

The kitchen is a cheery place today, cookies to bake, a crock pot of oatmeal cooking and an iPod full of holiday songs. How odd – and wonderful – to be in St. Paul, the Charlie Brown town, during the holidays. I remember waiting for *A Charlie Brown Christmas* to air every year.

If you want to see a group of college freshmen reduced to weepy kids, play the *A Charlie Brown Christmas* album in a dorm.

So here the kids and I sit, watching the snow and waiting for the cookie dough to chill thoroughly. We should just take it outside.

And we're waiting for Gerry to return from his Multiple Myelolma Support Group. This is Gerry's first MM meeting, a long time in coming, and he was pretty jazzed for it. He just called to say that there were about 22 people at the group, and the consensus was that he looks really good for someone who is about to have his Day Plus 100 appointment.

This was great for him to hear from other folks who are going this same route. My only worry is that the streets are getting mighty slick out there and I wish he were home now.

A few weeks ago he came home from grocery shopping – always a good time, by holding onto the cart he can scoot around without using his walker – and said that he was standing in an aisle and it suddenly occurred to him that he was depressed. It just came to him like an sudden idea. Which makes perfect sense, and I'm sort of glad that he came to that realization in such a simple way *(and in such a familiar environment as our grocery store...)*.

He IS getting better; every day he's moving more easily and seems to have more clarity in his thoughts. I see it, although it may be hard for him to judge. He can do just about anything he needs to, which makes him feel that he *should* be doing more. And that expectation leads to bad, worthless feelings.

Most of all, though, I can tell that he just feels so damned alone in this. And he still has such terrible back pain, which affects everything. In a weird way, we're back to where we were last Christmas – Gerry with a bad backache. But we've come so far. What a year.

I think that attending this group is the first step in dealing with all of the garbage he's pushing away. We've been so busy just getting through the whole MM ride, we haven't taken time to assess how that ride has felt. Since returning from Mayo, we've spent most of our time coming to grips with life with a traveling mom and a stay-at-home dad who isn't functioning at the level he'd hoped.

We haven't taken the time – we haven't *had* the time – to sort out our feelings about this year. One thing about going through hell, there's not a lot of time for introspection.

And, of course, along with all of these deep thoughts, the most important consideration today is where to go for sledding. Everyone has a glow on their face.

We've heard that Highland Park Golf Course is the best around here, so that may be where I take the kids. Gerry's been the family snow guy every winter, but this year the task will pass to me. I hope I am up to the challenge.

DECEMBER THIRD
ASSUMING THE MANTLE
ST. PAUL, MN

I was the designated taker-of-kids-to-the-sledding-hill parent this time, so I brought Atticus along for good measure. The kids had a blast on the hill back behind the Highland Park Recreation Center, and I ended up sledding myself. Atticus had an amazing run in a desolate area of the field, acres of untrammeled snow just begging for a dog to romp! We ended the day with lunch at Mickey's Diner, good times.

The State Rankings on Depression Status have come out, and the last two states I've lived in rank among the top 6 in terms of dealing with depression.

The top six are: South Dakota, Hawaii, New Jersey, Iowa, Maryland and Minnesota.

I don't talk about this much, but I am a proud member of the Fluoxi-team. *My name is Annie, and I take Serafem (aka, Prozac)*. I can't say I ever felt guilty about taking it, but at the start I did feel odd. Rather like I *should* be able to deal with anything on my own, without the need for chemistry to enhance my mood.

I was also worried that my creativity would be affected. That turned out to be a non-worry. Once I was able to prioritize my needs, wants and desires, I was more productive and creative. More than a *"happy pill,"* I feel that taking my pink and grey capsule helps me prioritize the important stuff, and allows me to let the other stuff take care of itself.

My dad was severely depressed – undiagnosed – and self-medicated using alcohol and prescription pain killers. Not great for him, and worse for his family. I have no idea what could have been done differently for my dad, given the treatment resources at that time.

But I have no doubts that my own life is enhanced by drug therapy. I know that my kids have a happier and more balanced parent than I did. So at least in that respect we're gaining ground.

Folks who are resistant to this – either for themselves or for others – can be very vocal in their disdain. It's hard to admit to taking Serafem when I know that some folks may say, *"Why can't you just handle a bad mood?"* or *"I don't think I'd ever rely on a* <u>drug</u> *to make me happy..."* But it's not really that way.

If you think of depression as a disease – and it is – then you begin to realize that taking a drug to maintain a healthy chemical balance in the brain is not that different from taking a drug to maintain lung health, or keep insulin levels in order.

But that's a big leap, especially if one has been brought up to believe that drug therapy for depression is wrong because depression is a weakness of personality or lack of willpower.

A few years I ran into a good friend who was dealing with postpartum depression. She'd had two babies in as many years, and was beside herself. She was also dealing with a husband and mother-in-law who felt that the only *"drug"* one needed to assuage feelings of depression or thoughts of suicide was a good religious foundation.

Religion can be a help and a comfort, but in this case my friend was made to feel guilty for even considering that there might be something out there that could help her bridge the place she was at mentally and the place she'd like to be.

I told her about my own experience, and she was very grateful to know someone – anyone – who had been going through was she was going through, and had found some light at the end of the tunnel.

Nothing in life is perfect, and I know some folks with mental health issues have been misdiagnosed and badly treated using incorrect medications. But for me this route has been working very well for a few years, and I'm very glad that I'm on it.

DECEMBER FIFTH

GELT ME, BABY!

ST. PAUL, MN

Life has escaped us this year in many ways. We're very focused on the day-to-day, and suddenly we look up and it's Hanukkah! *They keep moving that darned holiday...* So, in celebration, I made our family's traditional *(and rather self-consciously Martha Stewart-esque)* Gelt Cookie.

To "gelt" the cookies, I use any refrigerator cookie recipe – peanut butter, sugar, shortbread – or our family's traditional Nut Christmas Cookie. I roll the dough into 2" balls, peel the back off of a piece of gelt *(I prefer the chocolate JFK half dollar coin)* and smash it into the ball of dough to flatten it.

I leave the foil on the front of the coin, to be removed by the happy recipient of the cookie before eating. If the foil is not removed, then it's the traditional chewing of the tinfoil Hanukkah dentist visit... I bake these at 350° or until they're just brown at the edges. Let them completely cool before removing the foil.

We're meeting with the director at our potential new temple today – I hope she's duly impressed with our embrace of the little-known JFK Hanukkah Gelt tradition.

DECEMBER SIXTH

A MOST FRUSTRATING DAY

ROCHESTER, MN

Yesterday was part one of Gerry's Day Plus 100 checkup. It's the point when we return to the Mayo for testing and a doctor visit. And it takes place, as expected, 100 days after the stem cell transplant.

Thank heaven I had my new tiny rubber chicken with me, perfect for frustrating or stressful episodes. Squeeze it and it lays an egg. *I laid a lot of eggs yesterday.*

We learned that everything with Gerry is fine! He is recovering as well and as nicely as anyone can. His numbers are good, his tests were stable. *(We were told no change is good news, "Don't expect improvement, be glad if it's staying constant...")* Basically, Gerry is a textbook case of how a recovery should go.

Now for the frustrations. Which were actually not earth-shaking, just, well, nerve-wracking. We arrived at 10:00 a.m. for blood tests and a full body X-ray so they can compare his current state of bone to his previous state. Then off for the bone marrow biopsy, but for some reason we had to wait over an hour past the appointment time. Everything at Mayo is tightly scheduled, so this delay was pushing us farther and farther behind for the rest of our appointments.

And things got worse. The woman who checked us in came over to tell us that there had been a problem in X-ray so we had to return to have a shot taken again. She said, *"No big deal. Not really..."* Yes, really.

Then it began to snow. Hard. And everyone who walked into the waiting room commented, *"Wow, I'd hate to have to be driving in that!"* With every minute it was getting worse, and I knew we *would* be driving in it.

As time passed we knew we wouldn't arrive home when expected. Frantic calls were made to friends to arrange some kind of backup for childcare, but we're still so new in town that we just don't have a lot of backup available.

Nothing freaks a mom out like knowing that her nine and eleven year olds may be home alone, knowing that her husband is going through a painful procedure, and that there is still a two-hour trip in a Minnesota snowstorm.

I pretty much lost it. So many of the nerves of the past year came to a head in that moment. But I was able to walk away and freak quietly by myself. *Freak. Me. Out.* When Gerry got back from the biopsy, we still had a visit with the kidney doctor.

We were almost two hours late and rather uneasy. We didn't understand WHY we had to go see the nephrologist as we thought that Gerry's kidney function numbers were very good. It was unsettling. I knew we had to rush, but Gerry wasn't in a rushing frame of mind. *(Did I mention he'd been sedated?)* So I innocently suggested that he get in the wheelchair we'd been using as a walker and I'd push him to the next appointment so we could move faster.

And I met with the resistance of a man who's been stripped and poked and prodded with only his ability to walk propping up his pride. On top of all this, I was about to thrust him into a wheelchair and push him around.

I won. *(Don't toy with me, Landy.)*

We got to the kidney appointment and waited, and waited. Then we waited a bit more. I pondered running over to pick up the prescription for Gerry's pain meds, but I was feeling just pissy enough to actually think, *"Eh, let him stew for another half an hour..."* Lovely.

Don't you wish your girlfriend were a sadist like me?

I picked up the St. Paul paper that happened to be lying next to me and turned to – of course – the obituaries.

And what should I read but a moving paragraph about a 51-year-old man who'd lost his five year battle with Multiple Myeloma. The funeral was to take place a few blocks from our home later in the week *Very. Quiet. Freak. Out.*

So I ran over and picked up the drugs. Nothing like an obit to encourage kind thoughts.

We were finally called into the nephrologist's office where we – you guessed it – waited some more. Thank heaven we weren't near a window or I would have been counting snowflakes.

And now the knee-slapping, rip-roaring, HIGH-larious moment of the day...

The doctor walked into the room and basically told us that, after chatting with Gerry's doc, he determined that they'd gotten our files mixed up with someone else and Gerry didn't have to be there at all. *Freak!*

I think I broke the record for saying good-bye and thank-you-very-much to the doc, wrangling Gerry into the wheelchair and rushing to the door. We decided we'd leave Gerry warm in the lobby while I ran and got the car. *Good plan.*

As I reached the car I realized I'd left the keys with Gerry. *Good plan which was not well thought out.*

Suffice to say we got home a mere two minutes after Max, life is good, and our trip the following day for the second part of the visit was almost a total reversal.

We adore our doctor. She's funny and smart and said all the right things without fibbing or glossing over the hard parts. I wish she were a cousin. And speaking of cousins, today started with an email from my cousin, Jan, who is rather like a sister to me, and pretty much the last immediate family member I have, saying that her breast cancer has recurred.

Damn. I'm still trying to process this – I feel that I've been standing outside myself for much of the past year, and this just isn't sinking in. I deserve a day off.

DECEMBER NINTH

DISENGAGING

ST. PAUL, MN

I'm on antibiotics for this cruddy infection thing (the doc said it was good I came in because it was moving toward pneumonia), so I'm feeling a bit more worn out than usual. I went to bed early last night, but hovered online, reading blogs off of Gerry's laptop that I don't normally read. Multiple Myeloma blogs.

And I was surprised to find my own blog listed on a few pages as *"Gerry's Wife's Blog"* – which is definitely what it is. This year the blog has taken a turn; less knitting, more *life*.

I read about folks with this disease, spouses who are dealing with it. And, perhaps not wisely, but necessarily, spouses who are dealing with being alone. This disease is such a mystery. One blog written by a young mother (early 30s) surprised me when I realized that she and Gerry share a doctor at Mayo. She was diagnosed years ago, but is just *now* undergoing her stem cell transplant.

We had been told, but had not quite processed that Gerry seems to have a rather aggressive form of the disease. The huge amount of spine disintegration at such a rapid pace is unusual, and it seems that generally the disease is a little slower in other folks.

Or not. It's such a singular experience, this Multiple Myeloma thing. As in any important life passage,

233

comparisons to others can be as confusing as they are helpful. Everyone has their own experience, with their own way of coping and their own saturation levels. We can come together to compare notes, but ultimately we're solo on this trip.

Reading about other spouses who had their moments when they'd have to face the fact that no, we probably are *not* going to go poof in the exact same moment as each other when we're 88 after a long and happy life, is helpful. *Really.*

Yes, it's devastatingly sad, but it's less lonely than dealing with the folks who haven't experienced something like this, but insist, sometimes cavalierly, *"Of course Gerry will beat the odds, they're just statistics!"* They mean *so* well, and they are *so* kind, but their kindness is terribly expensive in how much energy it takes to absorb it and not scream.

Statistics are nothing on which to hang hope, or fear. Every case is different. But refusing to face the worst that could happen and calling it *"Positive Thinking"* is as unhelpful as saying that being brave means never being afraid. And this is a terminal illness.

Folks have commented on how well our family is getting through this. But I think it's because we haven't lost sight of the fact that MM, like life, is terminal *(to paraphrase Elizabeth Edwards).*

I'm afraid and I'm brave. I'm facing the future, accepting that the worst could happen, but I'm also hopeful and positive. Perhaps holding these complex feelings together in one mind is hard for folks who'd like to live simplistic single-emotion-at-a-time lives, but I can't do that. It's not how I'm made. We're all different.

So if I'm chatting with someone and they tell me, *"Everything will be fine."* I'll agree with them. Everything *will* be fine. But I may not mean the same thing that they mean.

They may mean, *"Gerry will make a full and perfect recovery, he'll live to be 105 and you'll have to legally change his name to Methuselah!"* They may try to cram our current experience into a single-emotion perfection that is easier for them to comprehend.

I, however, will mean, *"Gerry will live until he doesn't, but he will LIVE until he doesn't. We – his family – we'll live, too. And we'll use the love we share to pull us through the hardest parts."*

Life won't be perfect. But it will be *life.*

DECEMBER THIRTEENTH

JAX

JACKSONVILLE, FL

The flight here was uneventful; an exit row seat, excellent knitting (Hannah socks), and a new British History book on my iPod were the key to my joy. I only wish Gerry could be here to enjoy the hot tub at my hotel *(he got an okay to go into a pool from his doctor).*

Here I am, in my great and comfy hotel room, on TV is a festival of politics, and my knitting is laid out in front of me. Tea is brewing, I have some cookies, and I'm missing Gerry and the kids. At least I have some lovely decompression time before I teach tomorrow.

The absolute hardest thing about what I do is getting the professional Annie separated from Annie-the-buddy. Both Annies need time to "get over" a flight *(and need to have the space just have the meanies every now and then).*

If only I could have Gerry with me.

How I hate to waste time away from him teaching when it seems that our time together is so precious now.

December Twenty–Second
Home = Work
St. Paul, MN

This morning at 5:30 a.m. Gerry was awake – he now has this awful cold/flu thing that I had, and of course for him it's much more serious. He hadn't slept well all night, and since today's Saturday I gave him Nyquil and he's been sleeping all day. He needed it.

So he's sick, Hannah's had the same cough for two weeks now, but Max is healthy as a horse.

In a week when our solitary family existence is highlighted by the fact that we have no local family to descend upon for dinner and a good argument, I'm brought to tears by a local friend who just dropped by with cookies and her firefighter boyfriend to shovel our front walk. *That's almost moving into single-girl fantasy territory. It's definitely one of the nicest gifts I've received this year.*

But the best gift by far? This line from my cousin in WV whose breast cancer had recurred:

> *"The best news is that my surgeon said the lymph node and where it had metastasized was encapsulated so he got it ALL in one swoop!!!! And I only have to have a few radiation treatments to clean up what might be left."*

She called to tell me she'd be here to boss me around for as long as I can stand her. She's more like a big sister than a cousin. I can stand her for a long time.

December Twenty-Seventh
White Christmas
St. Paul, MN

I've alluded to the fact that it's been a hard Christmas for me this year, for many reasons, but mostly these last few weeks have been an emotional distillation of all of the fears, mysteries and joys of the past year.

What a year.

I ran into a very kind neighbor on a walk, and as we were chatting I found myself starting to weep. Not pretty weeping, either, but choking, sobbing, gasping, totally unattractive bawling that I've only engaged in so far in private, or in front of a class in Austin, TX. *(Hi guys! Mopped up that back room yet?)*

So it wasn't entirely a surprise when this very kind neighbor dropped by the next day to invite our whole clan to his extended family's Christmas dinner. And, having no shame, we accepted.

It was an exceptionally wonderful dinner. Aside from the good food and drink, the company was everything that Gerry and I had been longing for. Family is very important out here in MN; folks get together with their familial units at the holidays, and if you're solo, you can feel a bit out in the cold *(unless you throw yourself on the emotional mercy of a neighbor).*

Because Gerry's been so sick, because we're new here, because I travel so much and because we were away for an extended period this summer, we just haven't been able to make the connections we might have made had we been whole this year. So we are especially grateful to the White family for a lovely *white* Christmas. Thank you!

At least I was able to perform a parlor trick of picking up a dropped stitch on one cousin's sweater as she was wearing it, to the amusement of all. That kind of thing greatly impresses the non-knitters. *I do it in bars for drinks.*

DECEMBER TWENTY–NINTH
WILD!
St. Paul, MN

Max just got back from a Minnesota Wild hockey game with a friend from his Summer baseball team. He had a most amazing time and is absolutely glowing! Not only was the game a blast, but Max had a wonderful time with his friends, just being part of a group of guys doing a guy thing.

Max has missed that, the mental and physical rough-housing a boy can only get from other boys and a hearty dad. Max has had an emotionally draining year. Our friends were more than generous, and Max came home with a jersey, purchased so he would fit in with the crowd. *We should have painted his face.*

Sometimes I worry that his naturally sensitive nature – he's a very empathetic kid – will be too strongly affected by this year of turmoil. And what lies ahead. So I'm so grateful to my friend and her brother (and other male members of the family) who included Max in this boy-friendly outing.

I can't decide whether having the kids home 24/7 during Winter break has been draining, or whether Gerry's pretty much the same as he's been, but having extra bodies in the house has highlighted the amount of time he spends resting.

I can tell how bad he feels when he doesn't seem inclined to fix dinner or putter around the house, or toss a load of laundry in the washer. Not that we've turned him into Hazel or anything, but keeping busy is good for the body and the soul.

Gerry's going through a rough period of very low energy (he's had an infection recently), and he's not getting out and around as much as he would like to.

There's an ad on TV where folks sit around discussing the cost of dear ol' mom's interment, the point being that one should get insurance to cover these costs so your family won't have to have the same constipated look on their faces as the heroine of the ad.

The ad itself is annoying and guilt inducing. And it prompted Gerry to bring up the subject of *"What on earth will you DO with me when...?"*

We haven't discussed this so far. This is odd, and painful, and feels out-of-body. What on earth WILL we do with him? Or without him?

What are you doing the rest of your life?

239

DECEMBER THIRTIETH
A LIST OF GRATITUDE
ST. PAUL, MN

For My Blog Readers

Thank you to everyone who read my blog this year, to those who commented and to the shy ones who emailed me privately.

Thank you to everyone who vicariously lived through my own *annus horribilis*, and to those of you who helped me see that, in the words of Dr. Rachel Naomi Remen:

> *Sometimes what appears to be a catastrophe, over time, becomes a strong foundation from which to live a good life. It's possible to live a good life even though it isn't an easy life. And I think that's one of the best kept secrets in America.*

Thank you to Terese for reminding me to listen to this week's Speaking of Faith on American Public Media, where I heard the above quote.

Thank you – from the bottom of our collective hearts – to everyone who helped us weather this very rough year. Whether it was emotional, financial or fiber support, we would not have been able to get through this year in one piece without your love and help. Thank you.

Thank you to Minnesota for having us, for welcoming us, and for providing a lovely white Christmas.

Thank you to the Mayo for the gift of TIME. (Is there any better gift than that?)

Thank you to the many folks who are walking the same path, and have been in touch with Gerry and me, making us feel a little less lonely.

Thank you to our friends in New Jersey who saw our kids through a hard couple of weeks, and who so graciously accepted it when fate turned two weeks into one fun and lice-filled month.

Thank you to every shop, guild and venue that hired me this year. Words can't express my gratitude for you guys sticking with me and not bailing out when it became obvious that Gerry's condition was serious and might change at a moment's notice.

Thank you to everyone who saw me cry, rage or lose it in an odd way, and pretended you were looking at a sane woman.

Thank you to editors for allowing me some wiggle room on deadlines when life took over, and to my blog readers who afforded me a certain amount of slack because my mind hasn't always been 100% on my work.

Thank you to Gerry, who is my hero and my best friend.

Thank you to Hannah and Max who have more grace and maturity at nine and eleven than I had at 22.

And finally, thank you to anyone whom I've forgotten in my end-of-the-year stupor. I feel like I could do nothing but good deeds every day for the rest of my life and not pay back the kindness of friends and strangers this year.

Stay tuned for more fun next year. Because, when all is said and done, Gerry and I do have a great deal of fun, even in the middle of all the crap.

JANUARY FIRST
2007 INTO 2008
ST. PAUL, MN

So here's how we spent our New Years' Eve –

After dropping the kids off at a fund-raising baby-sitting evening *(they had a blast)*, Gerry and I headed off to the Grandview for a double feature of *Juno* and *Sweeny Todd*. Actually, we lost each other for the first film and sat separately, but during Sweeny we were happily holding hands.

And then the best part of the evening – picking up the kids, driving downtown and enjoying a very late night visit to Mickey's Diner. Fries and French toast and cheese sandwiches. I had a chicken sandwich. A girl with three shades of pink hair was sitting at the counter, and our waitress sang.

Back home we tried to watch the Times Square coverage, but we found it surreal and depressing, like a telethon, so we watched the Garrison Keillor special on PBS. That was much more fitting, and more fun. And then to our beds. *Or, actually, all of us to one bed.*

We all piled into our bed to watch *Mr. Smith Goes to Washington* and dreamed of the changes that 2008 will bring.

And thus ends a very hard year.

And a very wonderful year.

On to better things.

RED CARPET CONVERTIBLE DRESS & CORSET TOP

This dress was designed to grab attention moving down the red carpet. It's knit in one piece from the neckline down. The dress can be knit to any length you desire, from a corset top that ends at the hip to a full length, floor skimming gown. The neck is convertible too: you can leave the neckline as worked, or gather it to show some skin. The choice is yours.

Skill: K 3 Intermediate

Size(s): To fit Bust: 32 (38, 44, 50, 56, 62) "/82.1 (97.4, 112.8, 128.2, 143.6, 159) cm

Finished Chest: 33 (40, 47, 51.75, 58.75, 63.5) "/ 84.6 (102.6, 120.5, 132.7, 150.6, 162.8) cm

Total Length (Gown): 28.5 (33.25, 37.75, 43, 47.75, 51.25) "/73.1 (85.3, 96.8, 110.3, 122.4, 131.4) cm

Fiber: Classic Elite Yarns - Playful Weekend, (164yds /150m 1.75oz / 50gr) per skein. Color - Burgundy 10 (12, 14, 16, 18) balls

Gauge: 4.25 spi x 6 rpi over ribbing, slightly stretched, using size 8US/ 5mm 36" Circular needle (add'l needle size 10US/ 6mm)

Notions: Darning needle, 6 stitch markers. Size H crochet hook.

SPECIAL STITCHES

K2tog LS - Knit 2 sts together so they slant to the left *(aka SSK, k2togTBL or s1, k1, psso)*

K2tog RS - Knit 2 sts together so they slant to the right *(aka k2tog)*

VDD Vertical Double Decrease - Sl 2 sts as if to work k2 tog, k1, pass slipped sts over *(decrease of 2 sts)*

Cable Cast On - Adjust work so that all sts are on the left hand needle. Slip needle between 1st & 2nd sts on LH needle and pull loop through to front. Slip this loop onto the LH needle twisting it clockwise. Repeat, each time using new st as new 1st stitch on LH needle.

C8L - Cable 8 sts with Left twist - Slip 4 sts to cable needle and hold to front, k4, k4 from cable needle.

C4L - Cable 4 sts with Left twist - Slip 2 sts to cable needle and hold to front, k2, k2 from cable needle.

C4R - Cable 4 sts with Right twist - Slip 2 sts to cable needle and hold to back, k2, k2 from cable needle.

W&T - Wrap & Turn - Slip next st to RH needle, wrap yarn around stitch and return to LH needle. Turn work, sl 1, begin working back in the opposite direction from the previous row.

INSTRUCTIONS

BODICE

With larger circ cast on 140 (170, 200, 220, 250, 270) sts. Switch to smaller needles and work 2 rounds in garter st, then work Scalloped Edge Neck Chart 14 (17, 20, 22, 25, 27) times, placing marker between lace repeats if desired. Place contrasting marker to note start of round [center back]. Cont in lace pat, work all rows of chart.

Next 2 Rounds: Work Back Rib Chart around ALL sts.

245

Armhole Bind Off

Next Round: Starting at contrasting marker, work 27 (37, 42, 52, 62, 62) sts in rib as est.

Knit next 19 (19, 24, 24, 24, 29) sts, W&T. Next row (WS): Knit back across these same sts, W&T. Next row (RS): BO these same sts. Work next 51 (61, 71, 71, 81, 91) sts in rib as est.

Knit next 19 (19, 24, 24, 24, 29) sts, W&T. Next row (WS): Knit back across these same sts, W&T. Next row (RS): BO these same sts. Work rem sts in rib as est to contrasting marker. *Note: The back and the front do not have the same number of stitches in some sizes -- do not worry your pretty little head about it..*

Armhole Cast On

Next round: Work in Back Rib Chart as est to first BO section

Using a cable cast on, LOOSELY CO 19 (19, 24, 24, 24, 29) sts, W&T. Next row (WS): Knit back across these same sts,

W&T. Next row (RS): Knit across these same sts. DO NOT TURN.

Place marker (pm), est Chart B [Right Cable Chart] over next 8 sts, pm. Establish Chart C [R Dec] across next 2 sts. Establish Row 1 of Chart D [Front Bib Rib Chart] across next 31 (41, 51, 51, 61, 71) Establish Chart E [L Dec] across next 2 sts. Place marker (pm), est Chart F [Left Cable Chart] over next 8 sts.

Using a cable cast on, LOOSELY CO 19 (19, 24, 24, 24, 29) sts, W&T. Next row (WS): Knit back across these same sts, W&T. Next row (RS): PM, knit across these same sts. DO NOT TURN. Work in Back Rib Chart as est to end of round.

Start Bust Shaping

Next Round: Work Row 2 of Chart B to first marker (just past armhole cast on), sm, work Row 2 of Chart C across next 8 sts, sm, work Row 2 of Chart D across next three sts (2 sts + 1 st from

246

Chart E section, decrease of 1 st), work Row 2 of Chart E as established across next 29 (39, 49, 49, 59, 69) sts, work Row 2 of Chart F across next three sts (1 st from Chart E section + 2 sts, decrease of 1 st.) work Row 2 of Chart G across next 8 sts, sm, work Row 2 of Chart B to end of round.

Cont working in charts as established, dec 1 st each edge of Front Bib Rib [Chart E] until 1 st [Center Front Stitch] remains between cable charts - 110 (130, 150, 170, 190, 200) sts rem total.

Next round: Cont in Chart B as est to start of Chart C, work Chart H across next 21 sts, cont in Chart AB as est to end of round.

Cont working Chart H over Center Front sts, bringing two front cables together and joining them as charted while cont to work all other sts in Chart B as est - 105 (125, 145, 165, 185, 195) sts

Work even as established, cabling center front 8-st cable every 8 rows until work meas 3 (3.5, 4, 5, 5.5, 5.5) " / 7.7 (9, 10.3, 12.8, 14.1, 14.1) cm from point where cables join.

Note: If making corset, work to desired length then BO all sts loosely. If making dress, continue below.

SKIRT

Knit 1 round, removing all markers.

Next Round: Starting at Center Back contrasting marker, k10 (10, 10, 15, 15, 15) sts, (pm, k18 (22, 26, 28, 32, 34) sts) five times, pm, k to contrasting marker.

Next round: (Work to 1 st before next marker, YO, k1, sm, k1, YO) six times (do not work YO's at contrasting CB marker) Next 3 rounds: Knit all sts. *For a shorter skirt, work to desired length then go to Crocheted Edge.*

247

Rep last 4 rows until there are 72 (82, 90, 110, 118, 128) sts in center back section, 70 (84, 96, 108, 120, 132) sts in every other skirt section - 422 (502, 570, 650, 718, 788) Cont with no further inc until skirt length is 19 (22, 25, 28, 31, 34) " / 48.7 (56.4, 64.1, 71.8, 79.5, 87.2) cm from end of ribbing, or desired length.

Crochet B.O. & Edge
The crocheted edge gives the bottom of the dress weight for a nice swing.
With size H hook Bind

Off skirt as foll: (Sc into next st on needle, ch 2) cont around until all sts are bound off.

Cont with hook, (ch 2, hdc into next ch sp) rep around all sts in a spiral for a total of 3 rounds, or until crochet hem is desired length.

Crochet Terms
Sc - Single Crochet
Hdc - Half Double Cro.
Ch - Chain
Ch Sp - Chain Space

"CONVERTING" THE BODICE

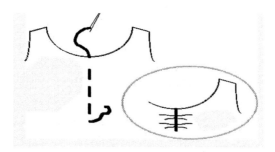

Using a double strand of yarn and a darning needle, run a gathering thread along the wrong side of the bodice, down the center front from the top edge to just above the cleavage point. Tighten gathering thread & tie together at wrong side of bodice. Tack in place, or leave tied in a bow to 'convert' the top later to a more modest look.

STITCH KEY

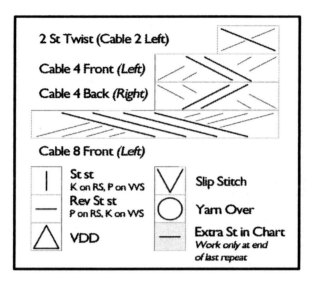

2 St Twist (Cable 2 Left)

Cable 4 Front *(Left)*

Cable 4 Back *(Right)*

Cable 8 Front *(Left)*

St st
K on RS, P on WS

Rev St st
P on RS, K on WS

VDD

Slip Stitch

Yarn Over

Extra St in Chart
*Work only at end
of last repeat*

Chart A - Scalloped Neck Edge Chart

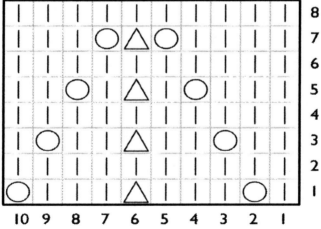

Chart B - Back Rib Chart

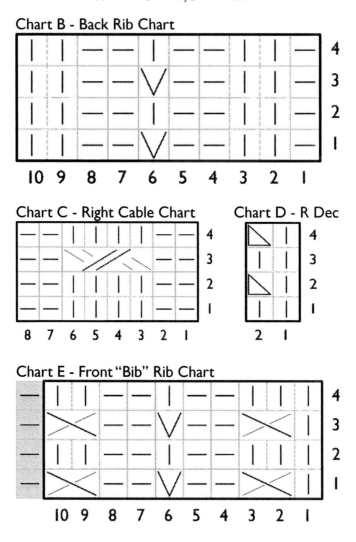

Chart C - Right Cable Chart

Chart D - R Dec

Chart E - Front "Bib" Rib Chart

Chart F - L Dec   Chart G - Left Cable Chart

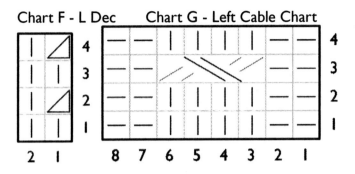

Chart H

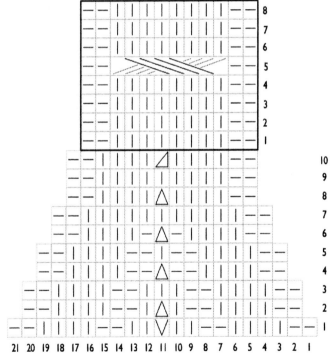

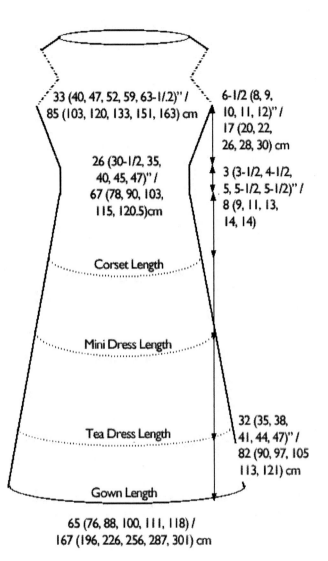

33 (40, 47, 52, 59, 63-1/.2)" /
85 (103, 120, 133, 151, 163) cm

6-1/2 (8, 9, 10, 11, 12)" /
17 (20, 22, 26, 28, 30) cm

26 (30-1/2, 35, 40, 45, 47)" /
67 (78, 90, 103, 115, 120.5)cm

3 (3-1/2, 4-1/2, 5, 5-1/2, 5-1/2)" /
8 (9, 11, 13, 14, 14)

Corset Length

Mini Dress Length

Tea Dress Length

32 (35, 38, 41, 44, 47)" /
82 (90, 97, 105 113, 121) cm

Gown Length

65 (76, 88, 100, 111, 118) /
167 (196, 226, 256, 287, 301) cm